RIGHTS
AND
RIGHT CONDUCT

by

A. I. MELDEN
University of Washington

OXFORD
BASIL BLACKWELL
1959

PRINTED IN GREAT BRITAIN BY
BILLING AND SONS LIMITED GUILDFORD AND LONDON

To

A. E. M.

ACKNOWLEDGEMENTS

A major portion of the argument in this essay was presented for discussion in a seminar given at the University of Washington during the spring of 1958; and the assistance provided by these discussions by my students is hereby gratefully acknowledged. In addition Professors Arthur E. Murphy and Alexander Sesonske have read the whole of the manuscript and have offered most helpful criticisms. No doubt I shall come to appreciate, even more than I do now, the weaknesses in the present essay; but for these deficiencies I shall have only myself to blame.

RIGHTS

AND

RIGHT CONDUCT

When philosophers discuss the term 'right', they do so almost entirely in respect of its application as an adjective (the right action); and when they have ventured to speak of its substantival use or uses in which it serves to mark the moral property of an agent (the right a person *has*), they have done so with very few exceptions by way of excursion from the main lines of their arguments. The immediate result of this is the unsatisfactory state of the subject of rights in the philosophical literature, for surely the complex features of moral rights in all of their variety cannot be elucidated in a few passing remarks. But there are other and even more serious consequences of this relative neglect of moral rights. Surely we do appeal to the rights which people have in the justification of action and from this it would seem to follow that any account of moral reasons will be at least incomplete unless due account is paid to the rights of persons. Indeed, discussions of right action which neglect rights will tend to err in other respects as well, for in neglecting the substantival uses of 'right', such discussions will ignore some of the complex features of the procedures of moral justification and offer an anaemic and distorted representation of our common moral understanding.

My ultimate objective in this discussion is to invite attention to relatively neglected issues in moral philosophy and by thus opening up the subject of moral philosophy help remove some of the staleness of a subject that derives in no small measure from the narrow compass within which arguments and counter-arguments have been confined. But my immediate objective is to explore some of the so-called foundations of certain familiar moral rights and the manner in which these operate in the moral justification of conduct.

I

There are occasions when the freedom of action of one person is limited by the actual or threatened interference of another and where there is the familiar challenge, 'By what right . . .?' Here the issue is not whether the net effect of such interference is beneficial, for it is not in general self-contradictory to say, 'I know that it would be useful for you (or him) to interfere, but you (or he) have (or has) no right to do so', but the standing or authority of the person in question. If, for example, A takes steps to go to the theatre and B acts in such a way as to prevent A from achieving his purpose, the dispute is not immediately at least over the question whether A's going to the theatre is beneficial or desirable in any way, but rather in view of A's right to go to the theatre if he chooses[1] whether B has any authority in the matter, a right, to interfere. For it is only if B does have authority and thereby the right to thwart A, that A's challenge, 'By what right . . .?' can be successfully met. A moment's reflection will assure one that the rights in question might be of many different sorts. (1) A's right to go to the theatre is not usually (although in special cases it could be) dependent upon some special relation to the performance or performers (he has provided financial backing for the show or his son is playing the lead rôle), nor need it depend in any way upon the fact, if it is a fact, that his going to the theatre would be enjoyable or otherwise desirable. In general, interested persons have the right to go to the theatre (surely, this despite the opinion of some religious fanatics is morally permissible) simply because they are mature moral agents capable of deciding for themselves how to conduct the course of their lives; but if it were morally desirable for A to go to the theatre he would say, less misleadingly, not that he has the *right* to do so but that he *ought* to do so. (It is trivially true that a person has the right to do what he ought to do, but to speak of a right in this case is only to provide a rhetorical flourish that derives from quite different and more central uses of 'right'.) There are innumerable

[1] It is not that A has a right to go to the theatre only if he chooses; his right is not conditional upon his choice. It is rather that A's right is to execute his choice of going to the theatre.

cases of rights of this sort: the right to go to the movies on Sunday, to choose his own neck-ties, to drink moderately, etc. In all such cases the actions in question are just the sorts of actions a responsible agent can be expected to perform without interference and as he chooses. And to say that he has a right to do these things in no way entails that anyone else has any obligation to ensure that he does so, but only to forbear from interference or coercion.[1] (2) But suppose that B has the right to prevent A from going to the theatre. This may derive from one or another of several conditions. (*a*) One can, of course, imagine cases in which A's going to the theatre would have disastrous consequences. If B knew that by going to the theatre A would expose himself to murderous assault but lacked the opportunity to warn him of the danger, he would be justified in attempting to prevent A from carrying out his intention, just as he would be justified in interfering if, having received the warning, A persisted in his folly. But we would hesitate to describe such cases as cases in which B had the *right* to interfere since such a locution normally implies that there is some special privilege or status on the part of the owner of the right. But whether or not it would be correct to speak of B as having a right, the propriety of interfering would be accorded any agent apprised of the consequences of A's intended action and does not derive from an authority or status peculiar to B. (*b*) One can imagine the sort of case in which B has been expressly accorded the authority to interfere by A himself. If A is too easily tempted to neglect his work by attending the theatre, he may well ask B to try to prevent him from succumbing to temptation, thus leaving to B to decide when he is to interfere. And if, now, having forgotten the request he made, A asks B, 'By what right . . .?', B's answer, 'You asked me to . . .' is sufficient. Here the right of B to interfere derives from the assent willingly given by A, and need in no way involve an explicit promise to interfere given by B, although, of course, it may do so. But when no promise is involved, B has a special right none the less. Now it may be tempting to try to derive such a liberty from the undesirable character of the action contemplated by A. But it

[1] Hohfeld in *Fundamental Legal Conceptions* (New Haven: 1923) speaks of the correlative of such rights as a 'no-right' rather than an obligation, and suggests in the interests of clarity that terms like 'privilege' or 'liberty' be used for rights of this kind.

is excessive busy-bodying to interfere even with our friends whenever they waste their time; and unless explicit authority has been granted interferences of this sort are usually unseemly and gratuitous. But when such explicit authority has been granted by A, B is privileged to act; indeed, he is duty-bound to do so.[1] I shall mention finally (c) the case in which B has a special right derived from his natural relation which he has to A as his parent. Now there are a number of observations I should like to make about such cases. (i) When B is parent of A, it is not the case in general that B's interferences are subject to challenge by A. Knowing that B is his parent, A knows that B is entitled to special consideration and to take measures on occasion which do limit his freedom. Hence when dispute does occur between A and B, it does not touch the question whether B has a special right, but whether the special right applies to the given case. A may claim that he has reached the age of consent and is no longer subject to direction in his everyday activities by his parent, or that while his parent has special rights in certain areas, they do not apply to the present instance since . . ., and so on. (ii) It is surely undesirable for parents and their children to make a moral issue of their relations with one another. Parents (and children too) may have rights but we prefer having their conduct guided by affectionate interest rather than by the thought of rights and obligations. (iii) Moral maturity is not reached all of a sudden along with moral independence. Children have obligations even when they are not quite capable of fending for themselves and of acting with maturity and moral independence. And even when they do achieve a considerable degree of moral stature, they do have obligations to their parents and the latter do have rights which they derive from their status as parents. (iv) The rights which parents have with respect to their children are various. Some are the rights which they have to guide the interests and conduct of their children (the use of the pejorative term 'interfere' would normally imply a degree of moral maturity on the part of the persons whose actions are affected), by choosing where they shall live, what schools they shall attend, and so on. Such rights *may*

---

[1] Such cases of privilege are to be distinguished from the liberty granted by A to B to allow the latter to read the former's diary. Here B is *not* duty-bound to read the diary. This sort of case is mentioned by H. L. A. Hart in 'Are There Natural Rights?', *The Philosophical Review*, April 1955, p. 187.

involve the correlative obligation of their children to abide by their parents' decisions (it would be impossible to draw any line marking the point in their development when children begin to assume *any* obligations to their parents), but they are also special rights in the sense of special liberties which parents have *as parents* and with respect to which others have the obligation not to interfere.[1] But (v) they may be special rights, not special liberties, the correlative obligations being not that of others not to interfere with their exercise, but the obligations which their children have *to them*. Among such rights are the rights of parents to special consideration from their children in indefinitely many ways and correspondingly the obligation of children to favour their parents in these same respects. Thus to return to our previous example, if A, by going to the theatre, fails in this obligation which he may have to his parent B, then even though B may not stand on his rights and although he may not even attempt to interfere with A's conduct even by such oblique methods as calling attention to his own interests ('I *would* enjoy the performance *so* much,' said longingly to A), which would suffer if A did as he intended, there would be a failure on A's part to meet his obligation.

Now I have not discussed all of the sorts of things called rights: *human rights*, if any, which are thought of as dependent in some way upon the 'nature' of human beings, or *general rights* which, depending upon the view one adopts concerning the existence and variety of human rights, have been distinguished from them, e.g. the right to speak one's mind, worship as one pleases, etc.[2] Nor do I intend that the rights mentioned above do justice to the variety of rights commonly involved in moral deliberations. I mention them in order to call attention to complexities generally overlooked when as all too often philosophers proceed hastily and brashly to offer summary formulations or definitions of the notion of a right. And, since I shall concentrate my attention upon one very special sort of right, I wish these preliminary distinctions and remarks to serve as warning against easy generalizations from the special sort of case with which I *shall* be concerned. Whether and to what extent

[1] As such, they are in Hohfeld's terms, 'no-rights'.
[2] Cf. H. L. A. Hart, op. cit., and W. K. Frankena's remarks.

what I may have to say about the special sort of right to be discussed may be applied generally to rights and liberties, I shall not attempt to decide.

I said earlier that I proposed to explore the 'foundations' of certain familiar moral rights and the manner in which such rights operate in the moral justification of conduct. I intended this remark to apply to the last of the sorts of rights I discussed above, viz. the special moral right which as we all recognize depends in some way upon an individual's status as a parent and with respect to which his son has the correlative obligation to his parent to *favour* him in his conduct. How is it possible that a right of this kind can '*derive*' from one's status as a parent and how is it possible for a right so 'derived' to function as a consideration that justifies the conduct of the parties concerned?

II

The right of a parent to special consideration seems to occupy a shadowy region lying between the matter-of-fact circumstance of being a parent and that feature of actions by which this right is honoured and to which we refer by such locutions as 'obligatory', 'morally required', 'dutiful', 'right', etc. On the one hand the *de facto* status of being a parent is to be distinguished from the moral right which the parent has. For (*a*) with respect to any special right of this sort, it makes sense to ask for the circumstance that provides the special moral title, and if so the right needs to be distinguished because it is in some sense derived from this circumstance. Further, (*b*) it is almost *de rigueur* nowadays to refer with approval to Hume's famous remarks in the *Treatise* (Book III, Pt. I, Sec. I) about the difference between the 'is' and the 'ought', in the present instance between the matter-of-fact circumstance of being a parent and the moral title derived therefrom. But the distinction thus drawn substitutes an embarrassing gap for a familiar distinction. How is it possible for a moral right to be derived from a matter-of-fact status? On the other hand, the right a person may have needs to be distinguished from the obligatoriness which, in a given situation, this right confers upon an action. For (a) the right of a parent may justify the special consideration paid to him. To cite the right is to cite a reason for the claims that an action, which honours the right, is morally required; but to give a reason for a claim is not to repeat or echo it. Again, if it makes sense to speak of 'demanding one's rights', 'asserting one's rights' or 'standing on one's rights', then we shall have to distinguish between the rightness of action and the right of the agent. For to demand, assert or stand on one's right (henceforth I shall use these locutions equivalently, departing if need be from ordinary usage) is to present one's warrant for the conduct demanded—it is not only to register a claim that the conduct demanded is right, it is also to present one's moral credentials, one's right, in support of this claim. Indeed, (b) the distinction is most clearly indicated by our familiar ways of speaking about the situation in which rights operate in moral discussions. If A, as a parent, has a right, then B, his son, has a correlative obligation. But this correlative obligation is not an obligation to do, but rather an obligation *to the other person*. It is only in virtue of being bound or having this obligation *to A* (notice: *an* obligation) that very *many* actions of B are reasonable and obligatory. It is the use of the same word 'obligation' (in expressions like 'obligation to do', and 'obligation to him') to cover both the moral quality of an action and the moral property of an agent that has given rise to confusion in most of the philosophical literature on this subject and has obscured the distinctive features of moral situations in which rights of some agents operate in restricting the permissible behaviour of others. By being under an obligation to one's parent, one's conduct is now restricted by the interests and desires of one's parents in ways which are both exceptional *and* reasonable. One's parent is thus endowed with the moral power to determine by his will and word the moral propriety of one's conduct and the moral integrity of one's person. But his will and word operate in this manner only because of his right, and unlike force and fear which explain conduct only by wringing it from us, a moral right justifies it.

Here, then, are two relations or distinctions that threaten to develop into unbridgeable gaps unless they are elucidated, one the relation between being a parent and having the right which parents have, the other between the right of the agent and the rightness of the actions called for. Clearly, no elucidation of the concept of a right of this kind will be complete unless both relations are adequately and correctly specified. But of these two relations, the former might well appear to be the more puzzling one of the two, for here there seems to be a world of difference between the *de facto* parental status of a person and his moral status as the possessor of a right, between the actual power he exercises upon his son and the moral power of his right. A 'naturalistic' reduction of the latter to the former seems implausible but the distinction between the two seems only to create paradox. The right of a parent does not seem to be logically implied by his parental status (how often have we been told that one cannot deduce matters of morality from matters of fact?) yet surely it is derived in some way from that status. Is it *causally* derived? What, if anything, would this mean? The difficulty seems to be even more acute than that pertaining to the manner in which a right can be derived from a promise one has received, for as I have argued elsewhere the notion of a promise is already invested with moral import,[1] whereas in our present case, the parental status of an individual seems to enjoy moral neutrality. But thus divested of all moral import, one's status as a parent can provide no intelligible basis for one's right; but of course this really cannot be true. The problem may be difficult but it is not impossible of solution; but instead of dealing with it directly, I shall adopt a more oblique approach by first discussing the manner in which a right which a person has may be related to the rightness of the actions for which the right calls. By showing how a right operates in the justification of conduct, I hope to be able to throw light upon the manner in which the right is derived from the given matter of fact, in our present example, the parental status of the individual.

[1] 'On Promising', *Mind*, January 1956.

III

A parent's right to special consideration can be honoured by his son in very many different sorts of ways; and by doing these things his son will meet his obligation to his parent. I shall now examine the question whether or not such obligation-meeting actions of the son are obligatory in the sense in which a failure to do what is obligatory is a failure to do one's duty and hence blameworthy (equivalently, a failure to do what is morally required in the specific situation in which the agent finds himself). In general, philosophers who discourse about rights assume that every obligation-meeting action is in this sense obligatory, so that whether or not they regard locutions about the rights of agents as replaceable without loss of meaning by locutions about right action, they assume that such locutions are equivalent. In any case they assume that it follows from the fact that an action is obligation-meeting that it is obligatory. They often express themselves as if they thought that if, for example, a person were to give up his theatre ticket to his parent and in that way meet the obligation which he has to his parent, then it would be his bounden duty to do so. Now it is this assumption that has led philosophers to hedge claims to the possession of rights with qualifications and even to heap ridicule upon those who subscribe to doctrines of 'natural', 'inalienable' or 'human' rights. For surely, they argue, we can imagine circumstances in which anything to which a person might lay claim as his right, must of moral necessity be withheld from him. So it is tempting to say, not that parents have the right to special consideration from their sons, but that they have 'presumptive' rights, the thought being that they will *have* rights only in specific circumstances and just to the extent to which these circumstances render the obligation-meeting actions obligatory.

This seems to me to be as confused and as mistaken a view as any in moral philosophy. It confuses two quite distinct notions—obligation-meeting action and obligatory action, and that these are distinct albeit related notions can be shown by means of the following considerations.

(1) We speak of a person demanding, asserting or standing on

his rights. Conceivably one could say 'I demand my right . . .' when one has no such right. Fraud and even mistake are possible, at least in unusual cases. Jacob asked for and received the blessing due to Esau and so A may deceive B into supposing that he is the latter's parent and thus stand on rights he does not have at all. Or, he may be mistaken: he is C's parent, but not seeing B clearly thinks he is C, and afterwards says apologetically, 'I thought you were C, my son.' Or, supposing neither fraud nor mistaken identity, he might make another sort of mistake and subsequently excuse himself by saying, 'I thought you could have met your obligation to me, but I see now that you were in no position to do so.' A parent can, in good faith, mistakenly demand his rights. But not only are such errors possible, one can also be ill-advised in employing the language and demeanour of one who demands his rights. It is not always the prudent thing to make an issue of one's privileged moral position and, when what is at issue is of minor consequence, one can be offensive in making an unseemly fuss about little or nothing at all. Indeed, cases of this latter sort are apt to puzzle us when we see them occur; we may not understand a person when we observe him standing on his rights about something trifling. What is such a person trying to do? And if no answer can be given, we should write him off as either mad or bewildering. But there are cases in which a person would be intelligible but morally unjustified in standing on his rights, when there is neither fraud nor mistake of the sorts mentioned above, when there is no disputing the relevance of the right to the specific circumstances of the case, when there is no question of prudence or distasteful fuss about trifles, and when, granted that he has a right that can be honoured, it would be morally desirable to waive, without losing or forfeiting, the right he does have. For a parent not only has a right *vis-à-vis* his son, but also responsibilities and obligations to him, not only a moral interest in the relations in which he stands to him, but also in the moral relations in which his son stands to others. Moral rights and their correlative obligations do compete for satisfaction. To favour one's parent in this or that situation *may* entail a needless sacrifice of the development of one's own talents or render it impossible to meet an enormously important obligation one has incurred to other persons. Surely it would be moral folly in such circumstances for a parent to stand on his rights and thus ignore the sometimes complex maze of rights and obligations that often surrounds all of the parties concerned. But if every obligation-meeting action is necessarily obligatory, it would be trivially true that one is morally justified in standing on one's rights, and self-contradictory to say that one ought not, by doing this or that specific action, to meet one's obligation.

(2) If every obligation-meeting action were obligatory, every case in which a parent waives his right would be a failure of moral nerve and a contribution to the moral delinquency of one's off-spring by encouraging him to turn his back on his manifest duty. On this view, moral apologies and excuses, not explanations, would be required in order to mitigate the blameworthiness involved in waiving one's right (perhaps, by citing the motive, 'It was a case of pardonable parental affection that led me to encourage him not to meet his obligation to me'), but we not only excuse or pardon parents for waiving their rights, we even praise them for doing so, and not only because of the otherwise commendable love and affection they display towards their off-spring but sometimes because of the superior moral wisdom they exhibit. If it is not self-contradictory to say that one is morally justified in waiving one's right, then it does not follow from the fact that an action is obligation-meeting that it is obligatory. If it is possible to be morally justified in waiving one's moral right, then we can state what would count as a case of this sort. And surely there are cases in which a parent would be morally justified in waiving his right, on insisting that, in the specific circumstances then on hand, his son must not meet his obligation to him, if by doing so he puts himself in moral jeopardy with others or sacrifices the development of his own talents. Surely, in other words, one may be morally justified in waiving one's right. Least of all is it true that one is blameworthy in waiving one's right.

(3) If every obligation-meeting action were obligatory then those cases in which rights (and their correlative obligations) compete for satisfaction present no mere practical problems to be resolved by the moral wisdom of the persons concerned but, rather, logical absurdities. If both A and C have rights as against B, then B will have obligations to both A and C. If, as it sometimes happens, B finds himself in a situation in which he can per-

form either action x or action y, but not both, then supposing that actions x and y are obligation-meeting with respect to A and C respectively, on the present view both actions x and y will be obligatory. If he performs action x, he will then be doing and not doing his duty; and the same holds true about the action y. It will not do to say that in such cases all moral bets are off on the ground that if he is morally damned if he does and morally damned if he does not, he is enmeshed in tragedy and deserves not censure but understanding and sympathy. Conflicting obligations are not instances of tragedy. Neither are they like instances in which all bets are off when the coin lands on its edge. They are, rather, familiar incidents in our common moral life which, in the great majority of cases, are easily comprehended by a not uncommon moral wisdom. There is no logical repulsion between rights or between obligations and it is, one must insist, the mark of the Pharisee to stand on all his rights, to view rights as if they were notes payable on demand, and obligations which one person may have to another as the inflexible decrees or air-tight directives of a quasi-legal tribunal.

IV

All of this might well seem to be a case of belabouring the obvious were it not for the persistent confusions with which the topic of rights is surrounded in the philosophical literature. Not only do writers commonly assume that every obligation-meeting action is a case of obligatory action, they often confound these quite distinct concepts. This is apparent in the attempt of Maritain, for one, to derive the right which a person has from that which he is obliged to do; for example, the right to life from the duty he has to preserve and achieve the fullness of his being—his good.[1] What precisely this means is not at all clear. What seems to be asserted is that I ought to preserve my being because that is good,

[1] Cf. *Man and the State* (University of Chicago Press), 1951, Chap. IV.

further that I have a right to do that which I ought to do, and since what I ought to do is to continue living, I have a right to live, i.e. a right to life. But this is in effect to translate locutions about rights into locutions about what it is right to do, and the best that can be said for this way of speaking (ignoring some of the curious steps in the argument) is that it simply ignores those areas of moral discourse in which we speak of a right which one person has *as against another* and, correlatively, the obligation which the latter has *to* the former. For what it substitutes for this language of rights is the different albeit related discourse about what it is right to do. It is this confusion that mars Bradley's discussion of rights and duties in his addendum to the essay 'My Station and its Duties' and, as I shall now show, much of the current talk about rights as claims.

A right, we are often told, is a claim.[1] But it is clear that since a person might have a right without registering a claim, i.e. claiming, we are to think of a claim as something a person has, whether or not he makes it, i.e. claims. Briefly, a right is a claim which a person may have even though he does not make it. But this surely renders unilluminating the statement that a right is a claim, for what on earth is a claim one does not make? Clearly, it can only be a right, and of course the word 'claim' is often used in legal contexts as a synonym for 'right'; but in that case we have not advanced a single jot. Surely, it will be replied, these writers are not simply advancing a synonym for 'right'. Of course not. If they were, they would not quickly add, as does Ritchie, for example, that the claim has to be sanctioned by society in the form of the approbation and disapprobation of private persons (in contrast to the sanctions imposed by society for the violation of the legal rights of persons). For the point of this specification is to distinguish claims that are justified and which, as justified, are rights from claims that stand in need of such justification and are not entitled, in consequence, to being designated as 'rights'. Thus it is that Garvin, to consider another writer, speaks of a moral right as a claim to something in so far as it is a just one. But such a move has the unfortunate effect of rendering the term

---

[1] By innumerable writers from D. G. Ritchie in *Natural Rights*, 1894, p. 78, down to textbook writers like Lucius Garvin in *A Modern Introduction to Ethics*, 1953, p. 478.

'claim' either too narrow or altogether unintelligible. Too narrow, because a justified claim would seem to be something claimed justly; hence no provision is made for rights that are not asserted —cases in which although A has a right to x, for one reason or another he or anyone else fails to claim x as justly his. (It will be noted that if need be I depart from ordinary usage in taking 'asserting one's right' and 'demanding one's right' to be equivalent.) Alternatively, if the application of 'justified claim' is to coincide with that of 'right', 'claim' cannot mean right; if it did, 'justified' would be redundant and in any case it would have the unhappy consequence of enabling us to speak of a 'justified right' and what this would mean is surely obscure. Would a justified right be a right the claim to the possession of which is justified? Every right is justified in this odd sense; that is to say, if whenever A has a right, his statement or claim that he has the right is capable of being justified, not by repeating 'I have the right' but by stating the facts which justify his claim that he has the right. Thus, if he has the right to special consideration from B, his claim that he has this right would be justified by showing that he is B's parent. By a 'justified right' one would mean, therefore, a right one actually has; so construed, the term 'justified' qualifies not the right that one has but the claim that one has the right. If, however, 'justified' in the expression 'justified claim' does qualify a claim as distinct from a right, then it is difficult to see what this claim could be if it is not the claim that an action is morally required or obligatory, in which case we have, once more, the familiar thesis that every obligation-meeting action is obligatory, this time in the extreme form according to which statements about rights are merely covert statements about right conduct. So it is in the case of Garvin's remarks. He tells us that 'rights are simply claims of individuals or of certain groups to certain goods and privileges such as are properly theirs in accordance with . . . social or distributive justice'.[1] Since, on Garvin's view, justice has to do with the apportionment of goods, i.e. with *doing* things in such a way that individuals receive and enjoy goods and privileges, the justified claim by individuals *to* such enjoyments turns out to be the justified claim *that* they ought to receive them. Put simply, the thesis is that to say that an indi-

[1] Op. cit., p. 479 (Garvin's italics are omitted).

vidual has a right to x is to say that it is right that the individual be given x. As this stands (although the difficulty might be rectified by counting a *possible* claim as a claim) this would deny that a person had rights unless he asserted them (or others for him), but asserting a right presupposes that there is a right to support the demand made. And it is by no means true that the possessor of a right must stand to benefit (to receive goods and privileges) from the actions that honour his right.[1] But the radical objections to this account of the matter are the ones cited in the preceding section of this essay. (1) Every justification of such a claim on the basis of the agent's right would turn out to be no justification at all, but an unavailing stutter. 'You ought to give me x, because it is mine in accordance with the requirements of justice', and this is only to say that 'you ought to because you ought to'. (2) One could not, on this view, speak of a parent having a right as against his son except in the case in which he was duty-bound to assert it and his son duty-bound to honour it. But it is not self-contradictory, it may even be morally commendable, to say, 'I have a right but I ought not to assert it', and 'I have a right to special consideration from B, but it would be wrong for B to give me special consideration at this time'. For, having a right is not the only consideration relevant to the claim that the relevant action is morally required. Hence a right may be waived without being relinquished or forfeited. (3) Every case of competing rights and, correlatively, obligations would give rise not to tragedy but to logical absurdity. The plain fact of the matter, too often obscured by the philosophical ruts that constrict our ways of speaking, is that attempted 'reductions' of statements about rights into statements about right action do violence to the actual procedures of moral reflection. Here we need to be reminded of Aristotle's observation that 'the truth in practical matters is discerned from the facts of life; for these are the decisive facts.'[2] And the facts do stare us in the face: Agents have rights. Rights compete for moral satisfaction. Moral wisdom consists not only in recognizing that a right may operate as a consideration that supports the claim that an action is right, but also in recognizing how to weigh such supporting considerations

---

[1] This has been noted by H. L. A. Hart, op. cit.
[2] *Nicomachean Ethics*, Book X, 8. Translation by W. D. Ross.

whenever they compete and how in such cases to arrive at a determination of what it is that one is morally required to do.

V

Of course I should not want to deny that when a parent says 'I have a right to special consideration from you', he may be claiming that it is obligatory that his son give him such consideration. When a parent utters such a sentence he may well be asserting his right, not reminding his son of the right he has. For if he utters the sentence in what might be called an assertive or demanding way, with the appropriate tone of voice, he is not only stating that he has the special right but also thereby making the claim that the obligation-meeting conduct is obligatory. An utterance of this sort may well have this dual or telescoped role, and this indeed is how quite frequently one asserts one's rights. Further, when this locution is employed defensively and to third persons in justification of the special consideration received, it may serve not only to specify the special right one enjoys but also thereby to defend as morally right the conduct which otherwise might appear to be odd or unjustified. Indeed, this dual use of sentences about rights is not restricted to first person present tense cases. But this is not at all surprising if we reflect upon the interest we have in statements about rights and the bearing which these have upon the moral character of conduct. For if statements about rights were stripped of their logical connection with statements about right conduct, we would have to say that we no longer had the concept of rights at all. To understand a statement about rights is to understand that this statement can be offered as a reason for the claim that the relevant obligation-meeting conduct is obligatory. To understand that such a statement is a reason is to understand that it can, in the appropriate circumstances, be decisive. And to present something as a decisive reason for anything else is surely not to remark upon an

interesting logical connection, but to present as fully justified
that for which such a reason is a good and sufficient reason. If
what is clearly at issue is some particular action x, by one's son,
one's statement 'I have a right . . .' is usually presented as a reason
for, that is, in justification of, the claim that one's son ought to do
x. It is surely unnecessary in such cases to add, 'It is your bounden
duty to do x and thereby meet your obligation to me'. The context makes this clear—spelling this out would be superfluous
rhetoric. So it is in the case of one who says, 'There are reasons
for believing p'. Generally one who utters such a sentence is not
making an interesting observation about evidence but recom-
mending that p be believed.

It may be countered that reasons for something need not be
good and sufficient. How then can saying 'I have a right . . .' (or,
'there are reasons for p') function assertively, as the assertion of
the right (or, as the assertion of p)? The answer clearly is that these
utterances need not really function assertively. Surely they would
not function assertively at all if one were to add, 'But there are
weightier considerations to be offered against doing x (thinking
that p)'. So one can, by the addition of 'but' clauses, take the
sting out of one's moral remark (or remove any suggestion of
conviction with respect to p). And this use of 'but' is revealing, for it does not preface a remark in which one merely adds
information to what has already been said, but makes it clear that
in this case, as distinct from the usual run of cases, the sentence
preceding the 'but' clause is not to be understood as expressing
the speaker's assertion. Normally the possessor of a right can be
expected to morally justify a given line of conduct by citing his
right. In most cases a right will make the greatest difference to
conduct: given the right, the conduct is justified; without it, it is
capricious and unreasonable. Hence unless a qualifying 'but'
clause is appended, the utterance of the sentence (together with
the appropriate demeanour, tone of voice) will be understood to
mark the assertion of the right. (And precisely parallel remarks
hold with respect to 'There are good reasons for believing p.')
The fact then that 'I have a right to special consideration from
you' can be used to express the assertion of one's right, the claim
that the addressee is morally required to meet his obligation, does
not entail that it is self-contradictory to say, 'I have a right to

special consideration from you, but it is not right that you give me such consideration here and now.'

The recognition that this latter statement is not self-contradictory has given rise to the distinction between *prima facie* rights and rights *simpliciter*.[1] What I have called a dual use of the sentence 'I have a right to special consideration from you' would, according to those who make this distinction, involve the claim to the possession of a right *simpliciter*. The use of such a sentence simply to state that one has a right or as a reminder that one has a right would, on this way of speaking, involve only the claim to a *prima facie* right. It would be self-contradictory, according to these philosophers, to say, 'I have a right to special consideration from you, but you ought not to give me special consideration in this situation' if and only if the right were an 'unqualified', 'absolute' right or a right *simpliciter* (these adjectives are often used synonymously); but because the right in question is to be construed as a *prima facie* right, no contradiction need arise. And whether or not one's right is a right *simpliciter* will depend upon whether or not there are competing considerations relevant to the situation and, given such competition, whether or not the right in question is most stringent. If there are no other morally relevant facts bearing upon the particular case, one's *prima facie* right is, in that situation, a right without qualification.

The best that can be said for this sort of distinction is that it does have a point: the fact that it might be morally objectionable to exercise one's right. There is many a moral slip between having a right and being morally justified in its exercise. But having recognized this much, those who contrast *prima facie* rights with 'absolute' rights or rights *simpliciter* thereby becloud it. First, the term *prima facie* refers apparently, not to the appearance of a right, but to an objective feature of the right, and this feature has to do with the possibility that the right may be 'overridden' by 'weightier' or 'more stringent' considerations in any given situation. But precisely what this feature is, and what the straight-

[1] Cf. William K. Frankena in 'Natural and Inalienable Rights', *The Philosophical Review*, 1955, p. 231; earlier in *Science, Language, and Human Rights* (University of Pennsylvania Press), 1952, p. 196. This distinction as applied to rights was introduced earlier by A. C. Ewing in *The Individual, The State, and World Government* (New York: Macmillan), 1947 (cf. Chap. II) and was borrowed from W. D. Ross's distinction as applied to 'obligation' or 'duty' in *The Right and the Good* (Oxford University Press), 1930, p. 19.

forward equivalent for these figures of speech can be, is surely puzzling. Hence it will not do to use such locutions in *explanation* of the fact that obligation-meeting actions need not be obligatory. It would be far better to repeat the point of the distinction than to obscure it by figures of speech for which no explanation is given except the desperate and unavailing appeal to intuition. Second, those who employ this distinction are guilty of confounding two quite distinct questions—the question whether a person has a right with the question whether, given that he has a right, he is justified by the particular circumstances in which he finds himself in exercising it. For it is no presumptive matter, something that appears on the surface but which might not be there at all, that a parent has a right to special consideration from his son. And the fact that he may not be justified in asserting it, or in believing that it would be obligatory for his son to favour him, does not qualify his right as presumptive or *prima facie* in any familiar sense of these terms, but rather the claim that this right ought to be honoured, i.e. that his son's obligation-meeting action is obligatory. There is nothing presumptive or *prima facie* about the right of parents to special consideration except in very special circumstances. I might not know, for example, that Smith, a parent, has conducted himself in a manner worthy of parents. For all I know he might have shirked his responsibilities to his son, and thereby abridged or even forfeited the rights which parents enjoy. But if this has happened it is exceptional; and where I have any uncertainty on this score, then I shall say that *prima facie* Smith has a right to special consideration from his son ('Presumably, he does have a right, but for all I know . . .'). But where I know that Smith is a person of integrity and has met his responsibilities as a parent, it would be misleading to say that he has the presumptive right, a *prima facie* right. He *has* the right which parents have *vis-à-vis* their offspring; and the right that he does have is no mere qualified one due to the special circumstances of misconduct or anything else. To qualify the right of a parent to special consideration on the ground that the exercise of the right might not be justified by the circumstances of a particular case is to paste the label on the wrong box. It is not surprising, therefore, to discover that Ewing, who seems to have been first in applying the term '*prima facie*' to rights, attempts to elucidate rights in terms of right conduct. For he takes 'rights of individuals' to be 'powers or securities of a kind such that the individual can rightly demand of others that they should normally not interfere with them'.[1] I shall not digress to comment at any length upon Ewing's failure to distinguish special rights of the kind I have instanced in the case of a parent *vis-à-vis* his son from rights in the sense of liberties (for this definition seems to have been framed with the latter in mind). What is important here is Ewing's explicit acknowledgement that he is defining 'rights' in terms of right conduct[2]—the right that an individual may have in terms of what it is right for him and for others to do or to abstain from doing. Small wonder that the introduction of the qualifying expression '*prima facie*' does involve the confusion of 'having a right' with 'being justified by the particular circumstances of a given situation in exercising it'. For now statements about rights are thought of as only slightly abbreviated forms of statements about what it is right for a person to do, but since, as it sometimes happens, the possession of a right may not constitute a sufficient justification of its exercise, the right which the person does have (no less than the rightness of the appropriate conduct) is now mistakenly thought to be in need of qualification as presumptive or *prima facie*.

VI

To distinguish as I have between the right of a parent and the rightness of his son's obligation-meeting action might well seem to be a case of substituting one obscurity for another, the present one for the intuitionist's talk about the weighing of *prima facie* duties and rights in determining which right and which obligation is most stringent. Given that a person has obligations not only to his parent but also to others by virtue of promises given, benefits

---

[1] *The Individual, The State and World Government* (New York: Macmillan), 1947, p. 10.
[2] Ibid., p. 11.

received and offices assumed as a teacher, say, or a member of the
medical profession, how does the obligation he has to his parent
operate in situations in which it is impossible for him to meet this
obligation in the face of competing obligations?

Instead of dealing with the question in these terms, let us
examine this sort of question as it arises in connection with so-
called moral rules. 'One ought to tell the truth'; but since a
physician might be called upon to deceive or mislead his patient in
order to save his life, the application of this familiar statement
conflicts apparently with 'Physicians ought to save the lives of
their patients'. To avoid the paradoxes of Kantism, intuitionists
hold that the 'ought' in these cases marks a *'prima facie* duty',
leaving the question of how the conflict between such 'duties'
may be resolved to the exercise of intuition. But how, if we are to
avoid this philosophical dead-end, shall we deal with such cases?

A familiar move takes the following form: 'ought' in the case
of these utterances is the 'ought' involved in statements by means
of which I say what in a specific situation a person is duty-bound
to do, e.g. 'You ought now to tell the truth to Jones'. (The
person addressed will understand me to say that it is obligatory
for him to do so now.) This specific statement differs from 'One
ought to tell the truth' in that the latter is doubly general since
the latter applies to any agent in any situation to which truth-
telling is relevant. Since, however, occasions arise in which one
may be duty-bound to withhold the truth, our doubly general
statement is expressed incompletely. It would be less misleading,
less inaccurate, according to the present suggestion, to preface
our doubly general statement with the phrase, 'In general, or in
most cases'; and since in general a person is duty-bound to tell the
truth (although sometimes the obligatory action might not be this
at all), moral truth is preserved and Kantism is avoided.

Let it be granted that on an exceptional occasion the obligatory
action might well be to withhold the truth, to mislead, but the
net result of the move designed to ensure this consequence is
disastrous. For as now construed, 'One ought to tell the truth'
presents us with a counterfeit as this is commonly employed in
our moral commerce. For this utterance is employed not in order
to inform us that in general or for the most part, the path of duty
coincides with the telling of the truth, but to guide us in the

specific cases in which we must decide what to do. If I knew only this much, that in most cases the obligatory action is truth telling, then so far there will be a doubt in my mind that in the specific situation in which I do find myself, my duty is to tell the truth. As a moral agent, I want to hit the moral target here and now and for this purpose the statement that I am far more likely than not to hit it if I do so-and-so will not serve at all. No doubt there are times when we must depend upon probabilities, take chances and hope for the best. In such cases there may be gaps in our knowledge of the relevant facts, but even here we do know what would resolve our doubts were the details of the moral picture to be filled in for us. Nor am I denying that there may be border-line cases in which, given all of the relevant facts, no clear-cut decision may be possible to which all intelligent and informed agents would assent. The difficulty on the present suggestion is rather that there must be a doubt even in the so-called clear-cut or standard cases. For if all that could be supplied is a statement of the sort proposed, then so far there is no method of resolving the doubt that must remain for any moral agent in every situation: 'Perhaps this is one of the exceptional cases in which one would be duty-bound not to tell the truth.' (Compare: suppose a bank clerk were merely told by his superior that in general or in most cases the cheques presented to him would be sound. He might then know that if he cashed a sufficiently large number of cheques, he would encounter few 'duds', but he must remain in doubt about any specific cheque presented to him unless he is given further instruction about the obvious precautionary measures employed by bank clerks to spot forgeries, etc.) If, now, thinking that what would make for a legitimate exception is the fact that a conflicting 'rule' is applicable, one might attempt a remedy by saying that one ought to tell the truth (keep one's promises, give special consideration to one's parents, etc.) in all cases in which by doing this no conflict with other so-called moral rules would arise. But this medicine is much too strong. Surely there are cases in which one ought to tell the truth even when by doing so one would be letting someone else down, and surely a physician ought to tell an occasional patient that his ailment is of no consequence if by doing so that will ensure his recovery. In any event it is precisely the cases in which rights conflict for satisfaction that pose the most interesting moral problems, but on the present suggestion there could be no moral issues in such cases. 'I ought to keep my promises' and 'I ought to give special consideration to my parents'; but if both of these specify what I am duty-bound to do on the proviso that they will not apply to cases in which either conflicts with the other, then I shall have no moral problem at all when I must choose between keeping my promise and favouring my parents. Surely this is preposterous. Or, shall we attempt to qualify 'One ought to tell the truth' ('One ought to keep promises', etc.) by an 'unless' clause: 'unless doing so would be morally undesirable'? This does reduce the statement to vacuity. Again, shall we attempt a qualification by listing the exceptions?[1] No doubt when we instruct children how to employ such statements in their moral discourse, we illustrate their use and, if we are wise, we provide examples of situations in which one might take precedence over another. It is natural to suppose, therefore, that in those cases in which truth-telling, for example, takes precedence over promise-keeping, we have 'exceptions' to the 'rule' about promises. But then, why not codify our 'moral rules' and state the exceptions? This is done, for example, in the case of the rules governing the bank teller's operations in cashing cheques presented at the counter. The teller is told that, subject to certain obvious qualifications, he is not to cash cheques drawn in an amount in excess of $50 except in easily specified cases x, y and z. But even if it were possible to do this kind of thing in morals it would substitute blind obedience for the exercise of moral judgement. Our teller follows the rules of the bank and he may do so whether or not he has any understanding of the wisdom of the directives that govern his actions behind the counter. He need only know the directives, recognize their application to given situations and perform his functions. And if a child is told, 'You are to tell the truth in all cases except those of the kind x, y or z', then so far like the docile artisan in Plato's republic it will be for him to do or suffer the consequences.

But it is folly to think that such a codification is even possible; or even that an order of precedence of so-called moral rules can be drawn up. Does promise-keeping take precedence over

---

[1] This is the move indicated, apparently, by Kurt Baier in *The Moral Point of View* (Ithaca: Cornell University Press), 1958, p. 193.

truth-telling so that it would be correct to say, 'One ought to tell the truth in every single case except those in which doing so would prevent one from keeping a promise'? Or, is it the other way? No answer can be given *in vacuo*. It all depends upon the particular circumstances of the specific case as to which of these sorts of action takes moral precedence. Shall I tell the truth to a Himmler and break a promise upon which hinges the fate of a group of Jews? Shall I keep my promise to a child not to reveal her whereabouts (she is playing the game of hide-and-seek) when her frantic mother, concerned for her safety, comes looking for her and asks me whether or not I have seen her? Surely it is preposterous to suppose that we can so qualify 'One ought to tell the truth' that every 'exception' can be foreseen and nothing need be left to the good sense of the agent learning how to employ such 'rules'. But this is an embarrassment for the view that statements of 'moral rules' are simply doubly general statements about what persons are duty-bound to do; for how, in the countlessly varied new situations that constantly arise, is it possible to discover what one is duty-bound to do?

At this point it may be urged that 'One ought to tell the truth' is after all only a rule of thumb and that the 'exceptions' are discoverable by applying some general principle, say, the greatest happiness principle in one or another of its well-worn forms. Time is usually too short and generally both knowledge and intelligence are too limited to permit people at large to estimate the consequences of any action with any reasonable degree of confidence. Moral rules, on this suggestion, embody the accumulated experience of the race; they can serve therefore as rules of thumb guiding our everyday actions. When they conflict—and these are the rare exception rather than the general rule—estimates of the pleasure consequences of conduct are decisive. Where no conflict occurs, these rules of thumb are good enough to be relied upon. Such is the move frequently encountered.

But now this does let the cat out of the bag! For now what we are morally required to do is really or strictly (everything else serves as a means if indeed it does) not to tell the truth, keep one's promise, or give special consideration to one's parents, but to produce pleasure, for this and this alone, on this monolithic doctrine one is duty-bound to do. I shall not pause to comment upon the irrelevancy of answering the question, 'Why should I keep my promise?' by saying, 'Because it will produce pleasure.' But suppose A favours B over C, the only moral justification, so-called, on the present view for doing so is not that B is A's parent, and as such has a special right, whereas C is a total stranger and enjoys no such moral privilege, but rather that by doing so in this case or in general, he will promote well-being, satisfaction or pleasure far more effectively than by acting otherwise. If by favouring C, A will promote pleasure more effectively than by favouring B, this and this alone will count and B's claim that he has a special entitlement in the matter by virtue of his parental status with respect to A will be dismissed as of no matter. It will not do to say, in reply to the objection posed by the absurdity of this consequence, that actions which favour parents do in fact maximize pleasure. No doubt parents would be distressed if their offspring treated them no better than they would total strangers, but their distress would stem from their sense not only that their offspring showed them no affection but also that their special rights were being ignored. In any case it is by no means obvious that meeting one's obligation to one's parents will maximize the general welfare. It need not make any difference at all in this respect and we can easily imagine contrary cases. Nor will it do to take Hume's line and argue that because all discourse about the obligations to parents would cease in circumstances in which utility were no longer served by such obligation-meeting action, the only reason for favouring one's parents is the utility of doing so.[1] For what Hume's argument shows is, not that utility is the 'sole foundation' of morals in the sense that it is the only justification of conduct that honours the rights of parents, but that in those imaginable circumstances in which utility would not be served there would be no conception of the moral rights of parents. Hume's argument repeated all too glibly by his present-day followers is an incredible logical blunder. One might as well argue that because one would not have yardsticks in a world in which physical objects were not solid, the only justification for employing them in the world in which we do find ourselves is the fact that objects are solid. This *does* obliterate the distinction between the

---

[1] Cf. Hume's notorious argument in *An Enquiry Concerning the Principles of Morals*, Sec. III.

point of a statement and its justification. No doubt, too, if chess-men were animated by powerful and capricious spirits that caused them to move in random ways on the chessboard, we would not have the game of chess and no conception of a chess move; but my reasons for moving this piece from this square to that have nothing to do with the physical stability of the chesspiece. So if we should live in a world in which reproduction of human-like beings were biologically unorthodox and the young were reared in queer cir-cumstances, there need be no utility served by favouring one's fore-bears, in whatever strange sense this term would then be employed, but equally there would not be parenthood, family or any of the moral concepts that surround these ideas. But we do have family life, the conception of a father and of the obligation of a son to him; and these concepts are involved in the moral justifications of conduct.

VII

Our interest in statements like 'One ought to give special consideration to one's parents' is logically relevant to our interest in doing what we are duty-bound to do in the various situations in which we find ourselves. Were we unconcerned to do our duty, we would be utterly indifferent to statements of this kind. But from this it does not follow that these statements are rule-statements which differ from statements about what given indi-viduals are duty-bound to do in this or that situation simply in this respect, namely, that they are merely doubly general in character, applying to any person and to any situation. It is only by supposing that this consequence can be drawn legitimately that philosophers have been led to speak of 'exceptions' to 'moral rules' and, in further consequence, to regard their ex-pressions as misleading or inaccurate, and even to suggest that general statements of this kind are only convenient rules of thumb. Surely we might do far worse than begin by sharing Kant's respect for a common and healthy moral understanding, and before resorting to these drastic measures, which in effect reject that understanding as spurious, seek first of all to render it intelligible.[1]

What needs to be emphasized is that morality, like science or any other area in which reason is exercised, is self-correcting. Misunderstanding and dogma are of course possible, but such defects can be removed by reappraising and reorganizing our thinking. It is doubtless true that for some people 'One ought to give special consideration to one's parents' functions like an air-tight directive to be followed blindly as the decree of the Almighty, just as it has been the case that axioms of mathematics and principles of physics have been accorded the hallowed status which, as subsequent reflection disclosed, they did not merit. In science, the consequences of these misconceptions have been ignorance, confusion and mistaken belief; in morals the bitter fruit of such constricted thinking have been the evils and tragedies recorded in chronicle and history and exhibited as dramatically necessitated in many a literary product. Antigone's unquestioning submission to the decrees of the gods must bring down upon her head the penalties exacted for the infraction of the laws of men. And there are present-day representatives of this type of submission to so-called moral principles who will bow to the despotic wills of their parents, no matter what the moral cost to all concerned may be, on the ground that 'One ought to give special consideration to one's parents'.

I shall argue, later in this essay, that in an important sense Kant was right in insisting upon the categorical feature of statements like 'One ought to give special consideration to one's parents', wrong, however, in the account he actually gave of this important feature; that in the sense in which such statements play a legitimate role in moral discussion, there are no 'exceptions' to them; and that it is, in consequence, a mistake of a fundamental sort to introduce the expression 'moral rule' to describe such moral statements. But in order to do this it will be necessary first of all to look more closely at the representation of moral reasoning familiar to readers of the philosophical literature.

[1] Even Kant, despite the rigorism to which he was led, remained firmly convinced that his statement of the 'fundamental principles of morality' was consistent with, indeed that it could be extracted from, our common moral understanding.

C

If, in saying that one ought to give special consideration to one's parents, one were saying that whenever any opportunity arises in which one could give such consideration, one would be duty-bound to do so, then the reasoning of a conscientious person might well assume the following form:

> Whenever any situation arises in which anyone could give special consideration to his parents, he is duty-bound to do so.
>
> Here is a situation in which I can give special consideration to my parents.
>
> Hence, here and now I am duty-bound to do so.

Given then that I want to do the right thing, I shall give my parents special consideration. But the objection to this form of argument, as we have seen, is the moral absurdity involved in asserting the major premise. It might be thought that this objection is peculiarly applicable to cases of practical reasoning about moral matters. That this is not so can be seen if we consider the familiar and reasonable remark that one ought to take baths. (Let us suppose that this could be expressed equally well by saying, 'Bathing is good for one' or 'Bathing is good for one's health'.) So one might be tempted to say that a person, mindful of the fact that one ought to take baths and considering whether or not he should do so now, could reason as follows:

> Whenever any opportunity arises in which one could bathe, one should hop to it.
>
> Here and now (in the public square) is such an opportunity.
>
> Hence, I should now hop to it.

Clearly there are all sorts of imaginable situations in which, if a person were to say, 'One ought to take baths', he would be making a sane and sensible statement, but the major premise of the argument as represented above is either silly or downright mad. And it will not do to say that what needs to be done is to qualify the major premise by prefixing the words 'In general' or 'As a general rule' to the sentence. What would these qualifying expressions mean? And how would they give us the force of the common assertion that one ought to take baths? Here there are difficulties that parallel those encountered in the attempts to render 'more accurate' the familiar statements of so-called moral .

rules. Will it do to say that one should take baths in all circumstances except . . .? Try to provide an adequate list of exceptions. Or failing this, shall we reduce our major premise to triviality by construing 'One ought to take baths' to mean that one should always take baths unless the circumstances are of such a kind that it would be folly, silly, useless or offensive to do so? And what would be meant by saying that 'One ought to take baths' is a rule of thumb? To be sure, if I suffer from some physical disorder, say some skin disease, for the treatment of which baths are prescribed by my doctor and I am told that I am to bathe at regular three-hour intervals, I shall probably do so without fail, but then I am under doctor's orders and my reason for acting as I do is not that one ought to take baths, but that I have been told by the doctor to do what I am doing. In this case a syllogism can be constructed that would avoid the silliness of the syllogistic arguments presented above. For now I can argue that I must take baths at three-hour intervals, and since my last one was taken three hours ago I must now hop to it. But even here there are proprieties to be observed which must be left for my good judgement to evaluate. And except where, in very special circumstances (e.g. I am in a hospital, attended by a nurse, etc., etc.), I am rigidly following the orders of the attending doctor, to construe 'One should take baths' as 'Whenever the circumstances are of the kind x, y and z, one should take a bath' is utter folly. Indeed, in such very special situations, the locution 'One should take baths' would not be employed at all; for this locution would be employed in order to advise someone how to take the necessary step to godliness or health; what would be said is something else again in order to make clear that one is justifying an unusual and quite strict régime to be followed by a patient.[1]

Now it would carry us beyond the scope of this inquiry to examine how it is that 'One should bathe' is actually employed by sane and sensible persons. But there is one important difference between this kind of statement and 'One should give special

[1] In her recent book *Intention* (Oxford, Basil Blackwell), 1957, p. 61, G. E. M. Anscombe remarks, 'Though general considerations like "Vitamin C is good for people" (which of course is a matter of medical fact) may easily occur to someone who is considering what he is going to eat, considerations of the form "Doing such-and-such specific things in such-and-such circumstances is always suitable" are never, if taken strictly, possible at all for a sane person, outside the special arts.'

consideration to one's parents' not only in respect of their subject-matter but, more importantly for our purposes, in respect of their logical features. I do not have reference to the fact that good habits will generally suffice for the former and that even where good judgement is required it is not of the order of that which is required by a moral agent reflecting on the complex moral circumstances in which he sometimes finds himself. Let it be granted that it is much simpler, requiring far less skilful exercise of judgement, being a healthy human animal than being an intelligent and successful moral agent. Much more to the present point is the following consideration:

One may justify in the appropriate circumstances the claim that one is doing what is morally required by stating that one is giving a special consideration to one's parent; but one does not justify the claim that one is healthy (let us assume that bathing makes for health, hence 'One should bathe') by saying that one has taken baths. One justifies, if one must, the statement that one is healthy by exhibiting the familiar signs of health, medical and otherwise. Yet one will bathe in order to become or remain healthy, and one can give special consideration to one's parent in order to do what is morally required of one. But the 'in order' in the second case is used in quite a different way from the 'in order' in the example of taking baths, not because it is a moral 'in order' (here one ought to reflect upon the unilluminating way philosophers have of speaking about a moral as distinct from a non-moral 'ought', as if this sort of remark promoted our understanding of the difference in question) but for a more immediately pertinent reason. Bathing preserves and produces health. Taking a bath is doing one thing, becoming healthy is something else again. A takes a bath at various times and only afterwards does he show the familiar signs of health. But giving special consideration to one's parents in this or that situation may be the very same thing as doing what is morally required of one. Hence it is that bathing may explain how it is that one has become healthy, but does not justify the claim that one is healthy; whereas in the case of one who has done what is morally required of him, the justification of the claim that he has done so might well consist in pointing to something that, in an important respect, is the very same thing as the doing of what is morally required, namely, giving special consideration to his parent. For in such cases, giving special consideration to his parent *is* doing what is morally required. He does not do the former in order to engage in another act; the very same thing described as 'giving special consideration to one's parents' is also described as 'doing what is morally required'. Because this is so, applying the former description to an action may justify (not explain as one would by showing how the thing explained has come about) the application of the latter description.

VIII

Let us see how it is possible that the doing of x which is in a similar respect the doing of y can justify the claim that y is being done. For this purpose I shall consider the following example: I make a present to a child by giving it a penny. I do this by removing the penny from my pocket and placing it in the child's hand. Let y be the action described as 'making a present' and x the action described as 'transferring the penny from my pocket to the palm of the child's hand'. Now I could do x without doing y. I might be teaching the currency to the child, showing the penny to the child, bribing the child, and so on. How does y—making the present—differ from these and from x—transferring the penny to the child's palm—when the very same action that is x is y and *could* have been any of the aforementioned actions? Here one may be tempted to suppose that the 'real' doing that makes x a case of y and not a case of anything else is something mental—this we do and when it eventuates in x, or causes x to happen, then we have a case of y. Alternatively, one might grant that the 'real' doing is y but succumb to the temptation to look for some concurrent mental factor and suppose that x plus this factor constitutes y. In either case one would suppose that there must be something mental going on (after all, whatever it is that one is doing in transferring the penny from one's pocket to the child's hand, the same physical operations take place[1]) and that it is the occurrence of this factor that justifies the description of the action given by labelling it as a case of y, rather than as a case, say, of making a bribe. But this will not do at all. It may be that what crosses my mind as I make the present is 'That will keep the brat quiet!' or 'What a sweet child!' or anything else you please.[2] Nor will it do to say that what happens at the time y takes place is an intention or purpose which occurs in my mind and which thereby makes x a case of y; for this begs the very question at issue by identifying purpose or intention with some mental event concurrent with the action x, and no mental occurrence of this sort could have the logical features of an intention or purpose.[3]

It is not, then, certain mental happenings taking place at the time x occurs that makes it a case of y, but the circumstances that surround x. Doing x, i.e. transferring the penny from my pocket to the child's hand may take place when I am making a gift (doing y), displaying an interesting coin, offering a bribe, making a purchase, teaching the currency, or whatever; and what is generally decisive in establishing which of these things has taken place need no more be what crosses my mind when I do x, than what crosses my mind establishes that I am promising when I utter the words 'I promise . . .'. The complex context in which x is done is usually decisive in establishing that what is being done is y, just as the moral context in which the words 'I promise . . .' are uttered is decisive in establishing that what is being done— the uttering of this sentence—is promising. For it is not only words and sentences that are understood, but actions as well whether these be the uttering of words or the actions we perform in making gifts, bribing, and so on. And these are understood not in the sense that causal explanations of them are given or that their effects are understood, but in the sense in which something done and described in one way is understood to *be* an action

---

[1] I shall ignore, for present purposes, the important question that is hereby glossed over, namely, how we may distinguish and connect the bodily movements that take place (movements of arms and muscles) from the action that consists in transferring the penny from one's pocket to the child's palm.

[2] For a more detailed discussion of this familiar doctrine, into which it is not possible to enter here, see my discussion in 'Action', *The Philosophical Review*, October 1956, and more recently the brilliant and decisive argument in Anscombe, op. cit., especially in Sec. 19.

[3] Cf. Anscombe, op. cit., on intention as something interior, pp. 41–49.

described in quite a different way. To have such an understanding of an action is to be familiar with and to take account of the relevant background circumstances that surround the action and thereby to recognize it for what it is. Given one set of such circumstances, transferring the penny *is* the making of a present; given other circumstances it is bribing, or paying one's tax, or making a purchase, or teaching the currency; but describing the action in any one of these ways is not stating the circumstances that are decisive in explaining what has taken place, any more than saying 'I promise . . .' is describing the circumstances in which this locution is employed in promising.

This is not to say that the superficially apparent circumstances in the context are always decisive in establishing that, when the penny is placed in the child's hand, a gift is being made. How, for example, shall we distinguish between making a gift and bribing? Here there are cases in which the agent's statement in explanation of his placing the penny in the child's hand may be decisive, just as there are cases when a promise is being made, the promiser's explanation that he is promising, not merely expressing his intention, will settle the matter. But unlike the case of a promise in which a simple statement ('I am promising') will be decisive, an explanation in the case in which one places a penny in a child's hand may be insufficient. Here the agent's thinking which he expresses in his responses to diverse situations and queries, and the explanations and justifications he offers to others, may be far more reliable than his express statement of what he is doing. Indeed, even self-deception is possible and one can, without dishonesty, suppose that one is making a present when in fact one is engaged in bribing. But even here there are ways of uncovering self-deception which are familiar to those practised in the art of penetrating behind the roles which we sometimes assume in order to display ourselves in a favourable guise to ourselves and to others. The point is that the circumstances in which placing a penny in a child's hand *is* making a gift are diverse, complex and sometimes subtle—they include all of the nuances of what in the broadest sense are the experiences and practices in the context of which what a person does when, for example, he performs the simple act of moving an object from one place to another is intelligible as the action described by the locution 'making a gift'.

It is now possible to see how one may justify the statement that one has given a child a penny by citing the fact that one has transferred a penny from one's pocket to the child's palm. For in the complex circumstances that do obtain in such cases—there is the elaborate institution of currency, gifts are made in recognizable ways by saying, 'This is for you', etc., etc., or simply by putting the gift in the child's hand when it has been wailing in distress (and this has happened before) so that it is now encouraged to run off in relief to purchase some candy after saying, 'Thank you!' and so on—one gives the child a penny by executing a requisite action, and granted these circumstances it is normally sufficient to justify the statement that one has made the gift by citing the fact that one has performed the requisite action, e.g. transferring the penny from one's pocket to the child's hand. It would be to misconceive completely the character of these proceedings to maintain that the justification requires a further premise, and that the reasoning should be displayed in the following manner:

> Whenever one puts a penny in the hands of a child under such-and-such circumstances, one makes a gift of the penny to the child.
>
> I put a penny in the hand of the child under these same circumstances.
>
> Hence, I made a gift of the penny to the child.

For quite apart from the easily exaggerated difficulty involved in spelling out the 'such-and-such circumstances', the major premise is not an additional item of information that is usually suppressed as in the case of an enthymeme, because as in this latter case it is obvious and hence need not be mentioned. On the contrary, it is otiose. For under what circumstances would one utter a sentence of this sort? Surely not in order to provide information about gifts to someone who already knows what a gift is, unless of course he is some visitor from another land who does not understand how the making of a gift is executed in this, for him a strange, community. (There, say, one puts the object at the feet of the recipient; here one goes through certain familiar motions.) But even in this case one utters the sentence, ' Whenever one puts a penny in the hands of a child, etc. . . ' in order to explain how gifts are made and thus explain the conception of making a gift which *we* employ (so that the person to whom this is addressed will recognize and understand what does take place as the making of a gift); and it is not that he already understands all that is involved in the conception of making a gift but is ignorant of some factual matter about gifts, e.g. that in these days giving a child a penny is not likely to arouse much enthusiasm. But for someone who has our concept of making a gift, and this surely involves understanding what would count for or against applying this description to action and thus being able to recognize what does take place when a gift is made as the making of a gift, the major premise is perfectly otiose; and the reasoning displayed in our syllogism is wholly misconceived. Given that I do put a penny in the hand of a child in the relevant circumstances, it *follows* that I am making a gift of the penny to the child. No further premise is needed at all. To recognize that the penny is being transferred in these circumstances is to recognize the action as the making of a gift. Such a recognition is not evidence for something being the case; it is, rather, understanding what is taking place.

One more consideration. We have seen how it is that citing the fact that x has occurred (transferring a penny from one's pocket to the child's hand) may justify the claim that y has occurred. Where the circumstances are recognized to be of the kind that x in those circumstances is y, citing x will be offering a good and sufficient reason for the occurrence of y. But the fact that x has occurred, while it is a justifying consideration in support of the belief that y has occurred, may not be sufficient. Let the circumstances be altered radically, and x in those new circumstances will not be a y, but, say, a case of bribing, and let the circumstances in which x in point of fact is a y be sufficiently obscure or uncertain, and the occurrence of x will not be decisive in establishing the occurrence of y. In any case x, the supporting consideration, may or may not be good and sufficient; but when it is, it is not because it constitutes decisive *evidence* for the occurrence of an additional event y, but rather because x in the appropriate circumstances just is the very same doing as the doing of y.

If the argument of this section is sound, and this is all that is being contended at this point, then the claim that, where x (giving special consideration to one's parent) is y (doing what is morally required), the justification of the latter by reference to the former might well contain logical features which have been ignored by moral philosophers. Let us now turn to a direct examination of this matter.

IX

Let us suppose that a particular person, A, abides by the wishes of his parent. The latter wishes him to do x and by doing x, A gives special consideration to his parent. Let us call A's action now described as 'giving special consideration to his parent', 'y'. Then A does x and by doing x, does y. It will not do to say that y is something that results from doing x—fulfilling the wish of A's parent. A might, unwittingly or inadvertently, secure the object of his parent's wish without thereby giving the latter any special consideration. To be sure if when acting in such a way as to take favourable notice of his parent's wish, A fails through accident, mistake or miscalculation to provide his parent with the object of his wish, then the description 'giving special consideration to his parent' will fail to apply to what he does. This, however, establishes, if indeed it does and then only at best, that securing the object of his parent's wish is a necessary condition of the application of the description 'y', i.e. 'giving special consideration to his parent'. The qualification 'if indeed it does and then only at best' is necessary, since if A's parent were ignorant of relevant facts or unwise, giving special consideration might well consist in not granting the wish of his parent. Nor is it merely that A must be concerned with the well-being of his parent no less than with his parent's wish; he must surely attend to the moral circumstances in which his parent is situated and even at the expense of his parent's immediate satisfactions seek to preserve or promote these features of his parent's status. Giving special consideration to one's parent, then, may be done simply by granting one's parent the object of his wish (and maybe not);

the former, y, is not something produced by x, the latter, as an effect. But while y is the very same action as x, y is x now understood in the enlarged circumstances in which it is performed. Granted, then, that in a given case by doing x, A does y and since y, in a given case, may be the same thing as the doing of what is morally required—let us call this 'z'—we now have a sequence of descriptions 'x', 'y' and 'z'. The doing of x *is* the doing of y and the doing of y is z. How are these descriptions related? I want now to concentrate attention upon the relation between the descriptions 'y' and 'z'. Here the relevance of the so-called rule 'One ought to give special attention, etc.' needs to be explored.

We have seen that it will not do to attempt to relate the descriptions 'y' and 'z' by means of some such premise as 'Whenever one gives special consideration to one's parent, one does what is morally required' (i.e. 'Every case of a y is a case of a z') —this being taken as the import of the consideration 'One ought to give special consideration to one's parent'; and we have also seen that the attempt to remedy the trouble by introducing qualifications only succeeds in creating further difficulties. Nevertheless, the description 'y' is connected with the description 'z', and surely the point of saying that one ought to do y is to remark upon this connection. In order to clear up this question, let us consider how this locution is actually employed in moral discourse. For this purpose I shall consider two quite different sorts of cases.

(*a*) An illuminating case is the one in which the locution 'One ought to give special consideration to one's parents' is addressed as it very often is to a child. Here of course moral training is under way and the immediate purpose of employing such a locution is to impress upon the child the importance of attending to the wishes, interests and desires of its parents. If a moderate degree of success has been achieved, the child will normally take these into consideration in its dealings with its parents. But suppose the child acts thoughtlessly and when reminded of its parent's wishes, says petulantly, 'I don't care'. Such a remark is not of course the dismissal of these wishes as morally irrelevant; nor is it an item of autobiographical information. A child wants this or that, and that it wants this or that is shown by its efforts to get what it wants. To attempt to thwart it in its efforts is to elicit an exasperated 'I don't care' and saying this is in some respects like a gesture of impatience with those who are meddling in one's private affairs. Here it is that the remark 'One ought to give special consideration to one's parents' will have an important role in communication. For such a remark can no longer be dismissed, along with 'Your parent wishes you to do such-and-such', as a consideration that has no bearing upon the child's intent (to which the reply might be made appropriately, 'I don't care. This is my business and if he wishes such-and-such, that is his affair'), for this new remark now serves to change the whole character of the discussion. The function of 'One ought to give special consideration to one's parent' is not to introduce new facts in addition to those previously cited (as it would be if one were to say that parents usually get their wishes, since if it were, an appropriate reply would be: 'How interesting! Perhaps yes and perhaps no, but in this case my parent won't get his wish'). What the consideration that one ought to give special consideration to one's parents does is to attempt to change the subject by putting the wish of the child's parent into moral relief. For what it does is to call the attention of the child to the moral context in which the wishes of the parent must now be viewed, thus forcing the child to consider them no longer as irritating obstacles to the attainment of its ends, which may be dismissed with a shrug or resisted if the parent threatens to interfere, but as moral considerations. And even if the child remains unmoved by the wishes of its parents, now understood not as mere impediments but as moral considerations, while it may continue to declare, 'I don't care', it will, if it understands what has been said, recognize that a defence, and no mere explanation of its conduct, is required and has as yet not been offered.

(b) Let us now consider the case in which a person *ab initio* is concerned to do what is right. Should he play golf with his friend as he had promised he would, or stay home and study diligently for his final examinations for which he is as yet unprepared? He weighs these alternatives and decides upon the former course, saying to himself that a promise is, after all, a promise. He knows that his parent is concerned about the uneven quality of his college work, but overlooks this matter, thinking that he might gamble on 'getting by' the examination and merely hope for the best.

Here the reminder 'Your parents would be distressed if they knew that you were neglecting your studies' might well play a crucial role. Let us suppose, indeed, that when this is brought to his attention, he decides rightly to stay home and study even at the expense of letting his friend down by breaking his promise. Now, does one need to 'connect' the fact that his parents would be distressed with the moral conclusion drawn by him via a premise that one ought to prevent such distress and thus give them special consideration? Surely such a premise is otiose; it remains unstated not because as in an enthymeme it is obvious enough, but because the connection has already been established by understanding that his parents would be distressed. To say that one's father would be distressed is not to say that one's immediate male ancestor (or the individual who provided the necessary means of fertilizing the ovum from which he developed) would be distressed; although unless some such account were true of the person referred to, he would not be described properly as his father. To be one's parent, whether mother or father, is to be a good deal more than one's immediate forebear (indeed, any item of biology pertaining to embryological development is not part of the meaning of 'parent'), and if by 'parent' one meant simply what is meant by 'immediate forebear', then so far there is no connection between the wishes of one's parent and what one is morally required to do. Indeed, so understood, there must remain an unbridgeable gap between these descriptions.

The present case parallels the case of 'I promised to do x, so I ought to do x.' Here it seems as if the connecting premise 'One ought to keep one's promises' is required. Now one would need to bridge the gap between 'I promised to do x' and 'I ought to do x' if by the promise one meant the uttering of the words 'I promised to do x' or their recognized equivalent (and it is difficult to see what else *must* occur when I promise). But so construed, how could the connection be made except by taking the promise-utterance as the subject of a prior agreement—a promise—not to use these words unless one will go on to perform the action x, thus merely postponing the difficulty?[1] And the same difficulty

---

[1] This is Prichard's predicament, as he himself recognized all too well. Cf. 'The Obligation to Keep a Promise', *Moral Obligation*, Oxford, 1948, and also my discussion of this point in 'On Promising', *Mind*, 1956, pp. 49–66.

remains if we tinker with the uttering of the words 'I promised to do x' by stipulating that these serve as the expressions of intention, predictions, and so on. The pattern is a familiar one. Just as it is that I understand that a gift has been made not by understanding simply that the object referred to as a gift has been moved from one place to another, so understanding that a promise has been made is not simply to understand that some such words as 'I promise . . .' have been uttered. And just as we understand the moving of one object to another in certain appropriate circumstances as the making of a gift, so we understand the uttering of the words 'I promise . . .' in the appropriate moral context as the making of a promise. But so understood, the uttering of the words (or their equivalent) 'I promise . . .' is already invested with moral import, and so understood no connection needs to be made at all between 'I promise . . .' and 'I ought to . . .'. No doubt I can explain to someone that whenever, in these circumstances, a person utters the words 'I promise . . .' he does bind himself to the person to whom he utters these words; but this is no more a connecting premise than explaining to someone that whenever an object has been moved from one place to another in such-and-such circumstances a gift has been made connects 'I moved this object from my pocket to his hand' with 'I made a gift of this object to him'. Such locutions explain what gifts and promises are, but once understood they are otiose. Hence it is sufficient to say to someone who has promised but who might not keep his promise, 'You promised'. To add 'One ought to keep one's promise' is in this case a superfluous rhetorical flourish.

So it is in the case of the allegedly required connection between 'By doing such-and-such I shall be giving special consideration to my parent' and 'By doing such-and-such I shall be doing what is morally required'. Knowing that I shall be giving special consideration to my parent by doing this or that is not identical with knowing that I shall be gratifying someone whose biological relation with me is of the familiar sort. Anthropologists have remarked upon the ignorance in certain primitive societies of the sexual role of the male, and how under these circumstances the concept of a father is unknown, but mere recognition of this matter of sexual fact and of the biological relation in which one stands to one's male parent is not enough to warrant application of the term 'father' in the sense in which this is employed in the expression 'giving special consideration to one's father'. Locutions like 'I have not been a father to my son', 'The man who married my mother was never a father to me', 'He was like a father to me' are neither self-contradictory nor absurd. They show that the concept of 'father' is not to be identified with the biological concept of 'male parent'. To make such an identification is to impoverish the concept of 'father', to create a mystery concerning the connection between 'giving special consideration to one's father' and 'doing what is morally required' and, in consequence, to pave the way for the desperate attempts to bridge a gap, created by our own misunderstanding, between these descriptions by looking for some general premise 'One ought to give special consideration to one's father'. And just as it is a mistake to attempt to connect 'I promised to do x' with 'I ought to do x' by means of a general premise 'One ought to keep one's promises' since given the recognition that one has promised, this general form of statement is otiose, so to attempt to reconstruct the moral reasoning from 'Here is an opportunity to give special consideration to my father (or parent)' to 'I ought to do so' by adding the premise 'One ought to give special consideration to one's father (or parent)' is to stutter. For the moral connection between giving special consideration to one's father (or parent) and doing what is morally required does not wait upon the introduction of a further premise, but already exists in the familiar moral use of the crucial term 'father' (or 'parent').

It may be necessary that if one is to promise one must employ some socially recognized locution like 'I promise to . . .' or some easily recognized equivalent, and it may be necessary if A is to be parent of B that A stand in the familiar biological relation to B. But neither condition is sufficient. Parrots, or imitative infants learning to talk, and mouthing the words 'I promise . . .', do not promise; and persons whose social functions are exhausted by the sexual acts whereby they fertilize the ova from which persons develop (whether or not this be done in primitive communities) are not fathers even though in this anaemic sense they may be counted as 'fathers' for the purposes of biologists or even in courts of law. But if they are so counted as fathers, their offspring owe them no moral debt and have no obligations to them. Much

more is required for the concept of a father (as in 'He was like a
father to me') than this matter of biological fact. A paradigm
case of a father is a male parent who plays his social and moral
role with respect to his offspring in the circumstances of family
life. Given such a context, one's male parent is a father. There is
then an enormous difference between recognizing someone as
one's immediate male ancestor and recognizing him as a father,
and there is no gap to be bridged between the descriptions 'giving
consideration to one's father' and 'doing what is morally required'.
Both are moral descriptions, and because they are so, the application of the former to an action may be enough warrant in the
appropriate circumstances for the application of the latter.

What then is the role of the utterance 'One ought to give
special consideration to one's parent'? Apart from instructional
purpose, the function of this utterance is to remind ourselves and
others of a matter of moral relevance to some desiderated action—
the fact that it is one's parent whose interests are affected and that
as such these interests are moral considerations that count for or
against the conduct in question. Kant was right, then, in insisting
as men of principle have always insisted that a consideration like
'one ought to give special consideration to one's parents' is
categorical. For there are *no* circumstances that warrant disregard-
ing as an item of no moral matter the fact that the interests of
one's parents are affected. This is not to say that in any imaginable
human existence, this condition must always weigh with a moral
agent. Let the family be extinguished or modified in important
respects and the concept of 'parent' is either impoverished or lost.
But given that there is the concept of 'parent' in the form in which
it is employed by us then it makes sense to talk as we do. And
the fact that by acting in such-and-such a way one will be giving
special consideration to one's parent is a moral consideration that
in the appropriate circumstances will establish the action as
morally required. 'One should give special consideration to one's
parent' is then categorical; the notion of exceptions is simply not
applicable here. To suppose that it is and either that there are no
exceptions or that there are exceptions derives from the confusion
of such considerations with rules or, as in Kant's case, with the
notion of Law. We have seen the confusions inherent in the
conception of such consideration as rules; it is scarcely necessary

to explore the confusion inherent in the phrase 'moral law' with its attendant obscurity, in Kant's drastically revised version of natural law theory, of the notion of self-legislating sovereign-subjects.

Why should it have been supposed that there are 'exceptions' to the 'rule' that one should give special consideration to one's parents? I venture to suggest two explanations. First, a perhaps hazardous historical explanation: such locutions are vestigial relics of an older view, no longer held generally by moral philosophers, of the source of morality—the conception of morality as founded upon the natural law imposed upon His creatures by the will of God. On such a view it does make sense to speak of violations of the law, of the command or requirement that one ought to give special consideration, etc., of exceptions that are or can be made for agents and by agents by God and by Godfrey. Here at any rate, the concept of exceptions does have an intelligible place, for logically, if not morally and theologically, it can hook on to the concept of divine commandments. For a command can be qualified by exceptions (this at any rate is logically possible) and here the notion of exceptions can take hold. But the modern talk of 'exceptions' to so-called moral rules attempts to preserve the logical feasibility of locutions about exceptions while rejecting the very conception of such so-called rules as divine commands on which this logical feasibility formerly depended. And even this half-way house is defective on still another ground. For a rule is something that can be laid down, established, contrived or devised in order to achieve certain ends, and where these ends may be best secured by introducing qualifications and exceptions, this is done familiarly and understandably. But no one has laid down or established that one should give special consideration to one's parents; and unless, as most of us are unwilling to do, we introduce God as the author of such 'rules' (in which case they would be more appropriately called 'natural' or 'divine laws'), describing 'One ought to give special consideration to one's parent' as a convention established by society, is either to assimilate such considerations to cases of traffic rules and/or to employ muddying language that serves only to conceal our confusions. Second, the talk of exceptions to such a consideration as that one should give special consideration to one's parents confuses two

D

quite different things—one, the fact that giving special consideration is always a relevant moral consideration, a reason for doing
the appropriate action; the other, the fact, if it is a fact, that this
reason is sufficient. For there may be exceptions to the normal
run of cases in which, in the appropriate circumstances, giving
special consideration to one's parent is in fact doing what is
morally required. Normally, the application of the description
'giving special consideration to one's parent' is adequate warrant
for applying the description 'doing what is morally required'. But
to say that there are exceptions to *this* generality is not to say that
there are exceptions to 'One ought to give special consideration
to one's parents'. For even where this locution is employed in
order to argue that doing what is morally required is the doing
that consists in giving special consideration to one's parent, the
moral rebuttal is never the denial that one should give special
consideration to one's parent. On the contrary, the reply is 'Yes,
but . . .' followed by consideration designed to show that because
of special circumstances this moral consideration is not decisive
in the present instance as it is in the generality of cases. And this
use of the 'but' clause is revealing. For it does show that the
locution 'One should give special consideration to one's parents'
is unexceptionable but is not decisive in establishing what is
morally required in the given circumstances. Hence the term
'exception' is pasted on the wrong box. It is one thing to be
justified in presenting the wishes of one's parents as a moral
consideration; it is another to be justified in claiming on that
account that the appropriate action is morally required. Exception may be taken to the latter, but never to the former.

X

In section V, I commented upon the mistakes fostered by the
confusion between 'having a right' and 'being justified by the
particular circumstances in a given case in exercising it'. It is

not surprising that this same confusion underlies the prevalent talk about 'one ought to give special consideration to one's parents' as a 'rule' that has or may have exceptions. For I have argued that there are no moral exceptions to the consideration that one ought to give special consideration to one's parents, given of course that the term 'parent' in its moral sense is correctly applied, since one is always justified in presenting the wishes, interests, etc., of one's parents as relevant moral considerations whether or not one is justified by the particular circumstances in a given case in acting in such a way as to give them special consideration. This result is not surprising, for the right of parents which I have been discussing in this essay is the special right which they have to special consideration, and viewed from the other side of the same shield, the obligation which persons have to their parents is one that they can meet only by favouring their parents in their conduct.

It matters not what word we employ to designate this unexceptionable 'One ought to give one's parents special consideration'. 'Rule' as we have seen is inappropriate and misleading. The word 'principle' has its own dangers. Perhaps most appropriate is Kant's own term 'maxim' which stresses the use of considerations of this sort in guiding conduct without suggesting the element of inflexible obedience generally associated with 'law', 'command', 'regulation' and 'rule'. To act on a rational maxim is to act on a relevant consideration, to be guided in one's conduct in a rational manner, and if we must plump for some descriptive term, Kant's word 'maxim' appears to be the least objectionable.

What is far more important, however, is seeing how 'giving special consideration to one's parents' connects with 'doing what is morally required'. I have argued that there is no yawning gap that separates the two, as indeed there would be if by the former one meant something like satisfying the desires (and so on) of one's immediate forebears. For 'giving one's parents special consideration' is already invested with moral import, not because it elicits emotions or pleasant feeling, nor because in some obscure way the use of this expression connects up in an *a priori* and synthetic manner with an unanalysable and exceedingly refined property, but rather because such a locution has the use which it has in a moral context and as such is already invested with moral import. Doing the things described as 'giving special consideration to one's parents' may be the very same things as satisfying the desires of one's immediate forebears; but they are the latter only in the circumstances of the familiar social and moral relations in which one stands to such forebears, and as such they are incidents not in the natural history of biologically related creatures but moral happenings. We need not be alarmed, therefore, by the weary ghosts that dance to every invocation of 'The Naturalistic Fallacy'—they have served their time by catering to our own confusions and should give us no further pause in this matter.

Just as soon as we think of the character of the intuitionist's move we must be struck at once by the extreme paradox of the position. If we ask 'What makes an action described as "giving special consideration to one's parents" a case of a morally required act?' it is tempting to take for granted that we understand the logical features of the term 'action' and to suppose that whatever difficulties there may be in answering this question are simply the difficulties, the uncertainties and obscurities involved in picking out from among those characteristics which actions, described in this manner, do have that special property called 'morally required'. And here our perplexity begins to deepen. How do I give my parent special consideration in my conduct? Obviously, in indefinitely many ways. I talk to him by long distance telephone, give him a ticket to the theatre, attend to my studies at the university, exhibit unusual generosity in my dealings with my brother, offer assistance to one of his close friends in whom I have no personal interest whatsoever, and so on. How very varied are the things that I do when I meet my obligation to my parent! Is it possible that one can find one characteristic invariably present in actions described as 'giving special consideration to my parent'? Here we are baffled and look, perhaps, for some more complex property, perhaps to the pleasures one affords one's parent. But even if this seems to be an attractive candidate—an illusion that ought surely to be dispelled by a little further thought on the matter—can we really *identify* it with the sought-for property of being morally required? For as intuitionists from Richard Price down to the present day have urged repeatedly, not even this will do, all other difficulties aside, since it makes sense to ask whether anything having the property of pleasing our parents is morally required. It is as if we began a hunt for a needle in a haystack, confident perhaps at first, but with a rapidly decreasing confidence in our ability to find it as we proceeded in our search, only to be told in the end that the needle was not there in the form we had imagined—shining, metallic and sharp—but rather in a condition and in a region forever shut off from our gross senses but accessible only to the higher reaches of pure thought. So whatever property we pick out cannot really be the one we are looking for, but only something else that is connected with our mysterious property in a most mysterious way. But if there is this much mystery about the whole business, surely we ought to be puzzled by the remarkable display of intelligence exhibited by the dullest of men when in their dealings with their parents they show any degree of moral understanding at all.

The paradoxical character of this search for a property is symptomatic of a radical misconception concerning one of the crucial concepts. It looks as if the problem is one of empirical discovery—if only one could find the required property! But this renders unintelligible the fact that people of quite ordinary intelligence have learned the use of the predicate 'morally required'. And whenever in philosophy the difficulty encountered in attempting to elucidate a concept appears to be one of the discovery of something elusive, something has gone wrong from the outset—we have become the victims of our own conceptual confusions. What has happened in the present instance is that we have succumbed to the temptation to make a very natural sort of mistake about some of the logical features of moral descriptions of actions.

We are not concerned with actions described as 'morally required' or 'right' in so far as they are purely physical or bodily movements, any more than we need be concerned when we consider questions of the propriety and excellence of the gifts we bestow on others with the purely physical properties of the gift objects, the bodily movements executed when we bestow these objects on others or even the property of exciting enthusiasm and arousing satisfaction in the recipients. I might, for example, give my daughter a diamond brooch on her birthday (supposing that this is within my means) and quite possibly this might please her far more than the modest article with which in fact I must content myself. But the propriety or excellence of the gift is a matter upon which much more than her or my own satisfactions or even the condition of my bank account depends. A great deal hinges upon the social practices of my particular set in matters of this sort and the fashions of dress and adornment observed by my daughter and the other members of her group. In the circumstances in which both she and I are situated, a diamond brooch would be an absurdly extravagant breach of good taste; in our present circumstances an inexpensive watch would be far more appropriate. To attempt to discover the excellence of a gift by mere examination of the physical properties of the object, thus ignoring this complex background of social circumstance, would be to launch into a wild-goose chase. Similarly, any attempt to discover the moral requiredness of an action described as 'giving special consideration to one's parent' which does not inquire into the social and moral circumstances in the context of which alone this description is applicable to any action, must needs make a mystery of such descriptive terms as 'morally required' and 'right'.

When we do attend to the moral context in which alone the description 'giving special consideration to one's parents' is applicable, the mystery must surely be dispelled. For in that moral context we have to begin with the institution of the family, the members of which are bound together by affection and common interest; in which perhaps, far more than in any other social institution, cooperation and mutual acknowledgement of interests are required for the effective maintenance and preservation of the individuals within the group and of the group as a whole. Within such an institution the natural relations of parents and offspring are well defined and within certain limits are associated in optimum cases with powers and privileges through the exercise of which the family life of the members is preserved; the children receive some of the most important features of a complex training and education that prepare them for adulthood, and the relation of parents to each other and to those outside the family proceeds satisfactorily. And there are, in addition, the moral relations in which the family and its members stand to persons and groups outside the family and in which, once more, the features of cooperation and mutual acknowledgement of interests are present. In short, to give special consideration to one's parents is to take account in one's action of their moral roles and of ours with respect to theirs in the common life of the family and the community within which the life of the family proceeds—it is to give persons so situated with respect to ourselves the special favours and attention by which we acknowledge their moral roles with respect to our own, and thus serve the common moral life in which in diverse ways all of the persons concerned participate. For the question of the rightness of an action described as 'giving special consideration to one's parents' is the question whether or not it serves and thus preserves the moral structure of the community. Hence it is not by minute observation of actions viewed in abstraction from this social process that the moral requiredness is discovered, but rather by the recognition of the manner in which the action described as 'giving special consideration to one's parents' can and does function within the framework of the common moral life of the parties concerned. In general, actions described in this way are also describable as 'doing what is morally required', although sometimes not; and no general formula is possible which would render unnecessary the employment of good judgement in determining whether, when the first description is applicable, the latter is also in order.

This may seem disappointing, merely a statement of what we have known all along. In a way it is, and in the end in that way it must be. How else could we get clear about the relation of concepts all of us employ so frequently and familiarly except by reminding ourselves of those features of these concepts which are revealed in our common discourse but which, in one way or another, we neglect only too easily when we philosophize? But in another respect there has been a gain—the recognition in our philosophical moments of these features and the sense that our grasp of these concepts is dependent upon practical features of our common life. These practical features are, to use a word I once employed, significance-conditions of the use of the moral expressions we have been examining, which escape us because they surround us and lie as it were at the periphery of our vision. To recognize that the uses of 'giving special consideration to one's parents' and 'doing what is morally required' are possible only in

a context in which those who employ such phrases are in varying
respects participants, either in fact or through the use of a little
moral imagination, that communication and understanding are
possible only for those who share, in Wittgenstein's happy
phrase, a form of life, this surely is no trifling unilluminating
matter that may be dismissed summarily as something not worth
the mention.

XI

In important respects, however, the remarks in the preceding
section are quite inadequate. We cannot rest content with general
remarks of this kind which lack all of the important detail
required in any satisfactory account of our subject. Further, a
good deal more needs to be said in order to make clear the
character of the connection between the descriptions 'giving
special consideration to one's parents' and 'right' or 'morally
required'. Indeed, the summary remarks in the previous section
must surely pose a number of questions in the mind of the
reader, which must be treated in some detail.

In the present section I shall deal with the question of the
relevance of consequences of actions to the determination of their
rightness. I remarked that conduct in so far as it serves and preserves the moral status of persons and the moral structure of our
common life is right. Surely this does suggest that considerations
of consequences are relevant to the connection between the
descriptions 'giving special consideration to one's parent' and
'morally required or right'. But here there are dangers against
which we must guard ourselves. In order to expose them I shall
begin by considering a question that might arise naturally during
the course of a game of chess. My purpose in dealing with this
question is to show how misunderstandings concerning the
concept of an action, even where the concept is applied in areas
outside moral philosophy, can give rise to error. I shall then

apply some of the considerations thereby obtained, to actions described as those in which special consideration is given to one's parents. In this way I shall attempt to make clear in what respects, if any, consideration of consequences is relevant to the determination of rightness.

Suppose the following question about a move made during a chess game is raised: 'Why did he move his piece to that square?' Let us suppose that the question is raised by someone who does know the game but who fails to understand what the player is doing. A number of answers can be given.

(1) He is carrying out such-and-such a strategy.
(2) He is forcing his opponent to exchange queens.
(3) He is check-mating his opponent.

In the first case the move is being explained by revealing it as one of a series of moves described in a general way as, for example, opening up his men in order to enable him to make maximum use of his available forces. To provide such an account is to provide an understanding of what the player is doing in making the particular move he made. It would be absurd in this case to say that the understanding thus provided is an understanding of the causal effects of the move that was being made. This is much more like the case in which 'Whatever is that man doing?' is asked about someone who suddenly breaks into a run after sauntering along at an easy walk on a crowded sidewalk; and the reply is given: 'He's drawing attention to himself in order to allow his confederate, who has the loot, to escape unnoticed. Clever, isn't he?' Here we have an understanding of what a person is doing by recognizing his intention and the background circumstances of the intentional action. And even if the agent's action, whether or not it is this case or that of the chess player, does not have the intended results ('The police are on to him and his confederate', 'His opponent knows what he is up to and will prevent him from executing his strategy'), two things need to be noticed: (a) the action will be understood even if the result or effect intended does not occur, hence to understand the action is *not* to make a causal inference, and (b) the idea of a result, consequence or effect in these cases is radically different from that involved in the sentence: 'The breaking of the fuel line had the result (consequence or effect) of stopping the motor.' One might attempt with some plausibility to fit the Humean conception of effect to this latter case; but nothing that is not ridiculous will ensue from the attempt to apply the Humean conception of an effect to the previously cited examples.[1]

In the second case, the talk is of 'forcing' an exchange of pieces. Here the idea of consequences is manifestly relevant. So here one may speak, granted the success of the manoeuvre, of the player forcing or causing his opponent to make the desired move. The difference between this case and the previous one is that while the notion of an intention is involved in both cases, here the intention has to do with a single move, the one made, rather than with a whole series of moves of which the one made is a member although, of course, the forcing move might itself be part of a general strategy being carried out. So it is enough in this case to speak of the move as a 'forcing' move in order to explain what the move is, whereas in the previous case one must, in order to explain that move, describe a series of moves in at least a general way, e.g. opening up the position of the pieces on the board. But while all of this may be true it would be a mistake to suppose that the words 'force' and 'cause' are being employed in anything like the sense in which we speak of one natural occurrence forcing or causing another. To be sure, if the opponent does not move in the anticipated way, the description 'forcing the opponent to do such-and-such' will fail to apply to the move actually made, but this does not establish, nor indeed is it even true, that in applying this description one is making a causal inference. Clearly, intentions, reasons, expectations are all relevant, but to treat these as interior occurrences standing in causal relations to one another and to the moves of the players is to adopt an impossibly simple-minded and distorted picture of the proceedings. That a game is being played, that rules are being followed, strategies and stratagems employed, that reasons of a special sort are relevant which need to be distinguished from the causes of the contractions of muscles as pieces are pushed about on a chequered board, in short, that a complex game is being

---

[1] Here, because of the limitation of space, I must rest content with the appearance of dogmatism, and can only refer the reader to my remarks on action in Sec. VIII, and to the bibliographical references given there on p. 32.

played and thus renders intelligible what is taking place as certain sorts of physical objects are moved about on a chequered board— all of this shows that the Humean conception of causality will not fit the use of 'forcing' or 'causing' in the locution, 'He is forcing (or causing) his opponent to do such-and-such'.

In the third case, the action described as 'check-mating his opponent' is, of course, intentional; but to say that the player is check-mating his opponent is not to state his intention (as in, 'His intention in doing that is to force an exchange of queens') but to state what he is doing, not by reference to anything in the future. Here all talk of consequences *in* the game is altogether out of place, although there might well be consequences *of* the game that is being terminated by this winning move, e.g. the payment of a wager. The point of the game is to enable one of the players through the exercise of skill, to gain a victory; to describe the move as 'check-mating his opponent' is to make clear how the point of the game has been achieved and by whom.

Now one could contrive a term like 'chess-required' on the analogy with 'morally required', but this is quite unnecessary since we do have a word that applies to both the case of chess and that of moral conduct. We speak of 'the right move to make' in chess and of 'the right thing to do' in morals. I shall argue that in both of these applications of the word, 'right' is a general term that covers a number of different sorts of things.

First, the case of chess. Consider the three accounts given above of a chess move: (1) 'He is carrying out such-and-such a strategy', (2) 'He is forcing his opponent to exchange queens', and (3) 'He is check-mating his opponent'. These descriptions can apply on different occasions to 'the right move'. But it is clear that while 'executing such-and-such a strategy' and 'forcing his opponent to exchange queens' *may*, in given cases and because of the special features of such cases, justify the application of the word 'right' to the moves so described, 'check-mating his opponent', if in fact it does describe a move, is never dependent upon particular circumstances as a warrant for applying the word 'right' to the move. The qualification 'if in fact it does describe a move' is of course necessary, the point being that even if the descriptions 'executing such-and-such a strategy' and 'forc- ing an exchange of queens' do in fact describe a move, it does not follow from this fact alone, as it does in the case of 'check-mating his opponent', that the word 'right' also applies to the moves made. It would be self-contradictory to say (extraneous matters of manners, morals or prudence aside) that it is not right to check-mate one's opponent. For the right move in chess is the one that does enable a player (if he has the requisite skill) to avoid defeat or to obtain a win by check-mating his opponent. One can debate the wisdom of a particular strategy or forcing move (whether or not this is part of a general plan of campaign), but one cannot ask sensibly whether or not the right chess move is the check-mating move. Yet it would be a mistake to suppose that the right move in the case, say, of the forcing move can be defined in terms of 'right' as applied to the check-mating move together with some such notion of causality, e.g. as a move that is either a check-mating move or one that will cause one to take place. (This is the analogue of the attempt to explain or define 'right conduct' in terms of some good to be achieved, e.g. pleasure, whatever *that* is taken to be, together with the idea of causality.) For (*a*) the idea of causality as applied to chess-moves ('What caused him to do such-and-such?') is *not* the idea of causality that is employed in the causal explanation of natural phenomena, and up to the present time at least this idea of 'cause' is surely one of the obscure notions that has not received the general attention it deserves. And (*b*) the chess move described as, say, 'forcing (or causing) his opponent to exchange queens' may be the right move to make even though there is no law-like connection between 'making the right move' and 'winning the game'. Indeed, the assertion that such a regular connection holds is patently false. I conclude, therefore, that while 'right' is intelligible when applied to chess moves, only by reference to the central notion of the object of the game—avoiding defeat and achieving victory through the exercise of a highly sophisticated skill—it is a general term that covers a number of different albeit related things.

The chess game situation is of course highly artificial and despite the complexity of the game differs from the moral situation in a number of important features. But in certain respects what I have said about the general use of the term 'right' applies, with a vengeance, to moral actions. This I now want to try to make clear.

Consider the series of descriptions 'granting one's parents their wish', 'giving special consideration to one's parents' and 'being considerate of one's parents'. I remarked previously that giving special consideration to one's parents might well take the form of refusing to grant one's parents their wish. Indeed, we can easily conceive of cases in which 'refusing to grant one's parents their wish', 'giving special consideration to one's parents' and 'right' will all apply to the same conduct. If granting one's parents their wish would cause them to suffer (they might wish for something which would be to their detriment), then denying them their wish and acting in such a way as to disappoint them might well be, depending of course on how one acted, both giving them special consideration and doing the right thing. Here, of course, the notion of consequences of one's doings may be highly relevant (but, of course, in the sense of consequences appropriate to actions, not the Humean effects of Humean object-events), just as the notion of consequences is relevant to the chess moves we make by which we execute our strategies and force our opponents, if we are successful, into their losing positions. So the notion of consequences of action is logically connected with the use of the description 'giving special consideration to one's parents'. But here there are dangerous temptations against which we need to guard ourselves.

Before remarking upon these matters, however, I shall ask whether and how the idea of consequences does connect logically with the idea of being considerate of one's parents. Now it is *persons* to whom the expression 'being considerate of one's parents' applies, e.g. 'John is considerate of his parents'. So employed the expression describes a commendable feature of an agent. It is sometimes held that this expression marks a disposition to act which can be expressed in a law-like statement about the actions of the person, to some such effect as that whenever circumstances in which consideration-giving action can be undertaken, the person so described will so act. Clearly, this will not do. It is true of course, that if a person is described as considerate of his parents, then one of the things that will count against the truth of such a remark is that he never acts considerately. But there are other things as well that count for or against such a description of a person. It may be that a person has changed and become considerate of his parents, or that in consequence of some traumatic experiences ceases to be considerate; but that he is considerate whether he has just become so or will cease being so is a matter not only of the relative externals of conduct, but of the character of his thinking as revealed by all the very fine shades of behaviour—tone of voice, facial expressions, manners, etc. Now that a person, characterized as one who is considerate of his parents, is commendable, that this is the right way for a person to be, is a matter with respect to which consequences of actions seems altogether irrelevant. It is tempting to say that a person's consideration of his parents causes him to act considerately, and hence that acting considerately is a consequence of his being considerate. This, however, is playing fast and loose with 'cause' and 'consequence'. For a person's considerateness is not an action, interior or exterior, which in the sense appropriate to actions, causes or has as its consequence an action. If a person acts in the way described as 'giving his parents tickets to a concert', then to say that he was being considerate to his parents is to specify a motive. But 'motive' here marks, not some internal occurrence in the agent's mind that sparks muscle twitches or anything else into being, but rather the character of what it is that the agent is doing. To use G. E. M. Anscombe's term, it *interprets* the action, i.e. it renders the action intelligible where before, let us say, it was not.[1] By doing this, it enables us to describe the action as one that is the giving special consideration to one's parent, or, as being specially considerate of one's parent in one's action. Now to be characterized as a person who is considerate of his parents is to be characterized as one who recognizes the special right of his parents, and to say that this is commendable is to assert a logically trivial consequence of something that is important, namely, that the person so characterized is mindful of or attentive to this right. To say that this is the right way for a person to be is to say that the right way for a person to be is, in this case, to be a person who recognizes the right of his parent. Clearly no reference to consequence is even relevant to the justification of this statement.

Let us now turn to the description of an *action* as one that consists in giving special consideration to one's parent, and to the question whether consequences of such an action are relevant

[1] Cf. Anscombe, op. cit., p. 19.

to the application to it of the adjective 'right'. Here, on first thought, nothing seems more obvious than that an affirmative answer must be given, yet nothing is less obvious on second thoughts. For everything hinges on how the action that is described in the very general way as 'giving special consideration to one's parents' is also correctly describable in still other ways. For (*a*) this is a very general description of an action, indeed it is only because an action is still of another kind—the action that consists in giving them tickets to the opera, being particularly attentive to one's brother's desires, and so on—that it is a case of giving them special consideration. To put it in another way, one cannot give one's parents special consideration *simply* by giving them special consideration, but only by doing something describable in a relatively matter of fact way; for if one says that one has given such special consideration, it is always relevant and appropriate to ask 'How?' In addition (*b*) alternative moral descriptions of an action described as 'giving special consideration to one's parents' may be given. Thus when I give special consideration to my parents by presenting them with tickets to the opera, I may in so doing break a promise to a friend since I may have promised my friend those particular tickets. So the action described in a matter of fact way as 'giving my parents theatre tickets' may be described both as 'giving them special consideration', and as 'breaking a promise'. These possibilities of alternative description complicate any attempt to provide a simple answer to the question whether or not the connection between the applications of the descriptions 'giving one's parents special consideration' and 'doing what is right' depends on the consequences of the action. Here we need to consider different possibilities with respect to the descriptions of action in order to avoid confusion on this point.

Suppose that the action is a purely private matter in the relations of father and son. The son has a theatre ticket but finds it difficult or impossible because of prior commitments to attend. The father would enjoy going, but so would an acquaintance whom the son likes but to whom he has no obligation in this or any other matter. Let us suppose, further, that giving his father the ticket would not be describable as breaking a promise or indeed as the failure to meet any other obligation which the son might have. Then in this case the action by which he gives his father the ticket to the theatre is also describable as 'giving special consideration to his parent', 'meeting his obligation to his father' and 'doing what is right'. It will be objected perhaps that the connection with doing what is right has not been established unless and until the consequences of what is done are taken into account. But what *is* being done? Of course it is true that one thing that is done when the ticket is given to the father can be described as follows: The son removes a printed rectangular shaped pasteboard from his pocket and places it in his father's hand. (Conceivably, one's interest in the proceedings might be of such a special sort that this description might come to mind: Prosecuting attorney: 'What did you observe?' Witness: 'I saw him give his father the ticket.' Prosecuting attorney: 'Could you see that it was a ticket to the theatre?' Answer: 'Not really; I was too far away. All I could see was that he took a printed rectangular pasteboard, etc.') This would be called a matter of fact relevant to the question whether the person gave his father a ticket to the theatre. For in the appropriate circumstances this matter of fact doing is the doing described as giving his father a ticket to the theatre. Now if the question is whether the doing described in the latter way is also describable as doing what is right, then questions of consequences are relevant. For if the son knows that one consequence of his giving his father the ticket to the theatre is that his father will enjoy himself that night, then all else being equal, the action described as 'giving his father the ticket' is also describable as 'doing what is right'. But so, for that matter, will be the question whether the action described as 'giving his father the ticket' is also describable as 'giving his father special consideration'. But if the action is described in this last fashion and is *not* also describable as 'failing to meet one's obligation to anyone', then no reference to consequences is necessary in order to establish that the action is properly describable as 'doing the right thing'. For the action so described is one by which the son maintains the social and moral relations in which he stands to his father. As in the case of the chess-move in which the description 'check-mating his opponent' is decisive in establishing the correctness of the description 'making the right move', so in the case of the action described in this way, the description given is decisive in establishing the correctness of the description 'doing the right thing'.

Suppose, however, that one way in which I could give special consideration to my parents is by helping them make payment on a loan they had obtained. This I can do by giving them money now in my possession which I can easily spare without suffering any hardship. Here again let us suppose further that doing this is unobjectionable, that this same action by which I would help my parents could not be described in any appropriate context as one by doing which I would fail to meet any of my obligations, legal or moral. Given this supposition, that is, *these* descriptions of the action, helping them make payment on a loan they had obtained will be decisive with respect to the application of the description 'doing the right thing'.

But 'helping them make payment' is itself a very general description of an action; for this description will apply to an action that is also describable in a variety of still other ways, conceivably, by means of the locution 'giving them the money I obtained through blackmail or murder'. And surely it is always wrong to perform an action describable in these sorts of ways. Here some might be inclined to say 'It all depends upon the consequences, when one blackmails or murders, whether or not one is doing the right thing', but this is certainly objectionable. For, questions of decencies aside, it suggests that what is 'really' involved in these sorts of description is, *qua* description, some morally neutral description. The thought here is that murder, for example, is really killing of a certain kind (which by itself does not seem decisive in establishing the actions to which this item is applied as wrong, since one can do this sort of thing in times of war on the battlefield without exposing oneself to moral censure), which may or may not be justified and which, when unjustified, is labelled 'murder' in order to convey a kind of moral 'Bah!' What is important, it will be argued, is the description 'getting money obtained through (say) killing' and this, if unjustified, can be shown to be unjustified by reference to consequences either of this particular action or of the class of action of this sort. The former alternative need not now be considered, it is much more fashionable these days to adopt the latter move. But which *is* the class of actions in question, that is to say, in terms of what

E

description shall we pick out the relevant sort of action? For the action was first described as 'helping them make payment' and then as 'giving them the money I obtained through murder' and, then, in order to achieve 'purity' of description, as 'giving them the money I obtained through killing'. But the same action could also be described in greater detail as 'giving them the money I obtained through killing my wife' and even more so by means of the expression 'giving them the money I obtained through the killing of my wife and the sale of her body to the animal-fat rendering establishment'. There need be no early stopping in the series of descriptions of the same action as more and more circumstances (including those that are morally offensive) that surround the action are brought into the picture, and if the action is described in such a way that it is logically impossible to apply it to an action without thereby labelling it as one that is destructive of the moral relations that hold between persons, then no appeal to consequences is relevant. For it is not a 'matter of fact' consequence that an action given the morally offensive description just cited has morally undesirable consequences (it might of course have other consequences that are unfortunate, e.g. I shall get caught and be hung, which would serve me right were I to do this sort of thing)—it is not logically possible to have actions of the sort in which the moral relations of husband and wife are maintained.

The example is of course fantastic, but we need not depend solely upon it for our argument. Let us return, therefore, to the previously suggested reconstruction of the description 'giving them money obtained through murder' into 'giving them money obtained through killing of such-and-such a sort'. Here, the thought underlying this move is to obtain a correct and 'really proper' description, that the unreconstructed description is somewhat misleading since it serves to convey our moral verdict and hence involves something more than mere description, and, finally, that the moral verdict itself is justified, if at all, only by an appeal to the consequences of actions having the 'correct' or 'proper' description.

Here my objection is not the verbal one that 'murder' in ordinary usage is called a 'descriptive' term. Nor is my contention the merely verbal one that an appeal to consequences in the case of 'This is murder' is unnecessary since in familiar use of the term the description 'murder', when used in such a sentence, is decisive in establishing that the action referred to is wrong. For, of course, one might reply by saying that all of this begs the question, since in order to know that the action is a case of murder we need to know that the consequences of the kind of killing done are morally undesirable. What is at issue is the allegedly 'pure description' conveyed by a phrase of the form 'killing of such-and-such a kind'. But here, again, the relevant question to ask is 'which description shall we take as the "purely factual description"?' Let us start by saying that murder is the wilful and deliberate killing of another human being—this in point of fact is given as a definition in a standard dictionary. But this, however, is scarcely the description of the desired factual purity; for what will count as an act that is wilful is not merely a voluntary act (if it did, the word 'deliberate' by itself would suffice) but one that is morally perverse in that the agent under-stands but flouts the reasonable considerations that would stay the hand of another. In any case, it is the killing of another human being who counts as a moral agent, a person, not the kind of living organism which exhibits those characteristics with which a biologist would be concerned. What those biological characteristics are I am now quite uncertain, and no doubt, for I do trust biologists in this matter, their description of a human being would apply to any being whom I would recognize as a person. But the concept of a human being as employed by the biologist is not my concept of a human being, and the relation between these distinct concepts can be indicated by saying that anything that would count as a human being in my sense, a sense involved in the dictionary definition of the word 'murder', would need to be much more than a biological organism; specifically he would need to be actually (or potentially as an infant) a social and moral being. As Locke once remarked about the term 'person', so we can say of the term 'human being' that it is a forensic term that applies to beings who are morally concerned and morally accountable.

If we were to strip the dictionary definition of all moral import, should we not have to describe the proceedings, which we do in fact describe as murder, in some such manner in which this is done by a natural scientist, say a physiologist? If an action is wilful and deliberate, it is one performed by an agent who can give and recognize reasons including moral reasons for his conduct, but who in this instance flouts considerations that would be relevant to the condemnation of his action. If an action is the doing of something with respect to another human being, it is the doing of something with respect to a being of like sort—a person with whom one does or can have moral relations of some kind or other. To avoid any moral implications of any sort, let it then be the physiologist's account of the proceedings which serves as the very model of a purely descriptive statement. In that case, however, we no longer have talk about actions, but rather about muscle twitches, nerve impulses and the like, about which our knowledge is surely obscure and problematical—features that do *not* hold true of our deliberate actions. 'Purity of description' has been achieved only by changing the subject.

It is true, of course, that if some general account given by a physiologist did not apply to what happens when a person performs an action, then the description 'killing a human being wilfully and deliberately' would also fail to apply. But to say that this latter locution describes some happening is not to offer anything like the physiologist's account. For it is only if the events described by the physiologist take place in the appropriate context—a context in which the elaborate physiological mechanisms, whatever they may be, are treated as the mechanisms of the body of a person who stands in a variety of social and moral relations to other persons, in which accordingly the muscles twitch and move, however they do this, in the performance of an action, that we have what can be described as a murder, the killing of a human being wilfully and deliberately. In matters of human fact, the term 'matter of fact' is a relative term and so is the term 'description', for there are all sorts of matter of facts (and descriptions, too) and what will be called a 'matter of fact' will depend upon what is at issue.

Consider the following account of the happenings involved in the killing of another human being. 'The bullet left the gun at such-and-such a distance, entering the body at such-and-such a point and angle, penetrating the heart, thus causing death.' The conclusion to which this matter of fact account might give rise is that someone unknown killed Smith by shooting him. This conclusion introduces us at once to forensic matters, to use Locke's apt term, hence the matter of fact description given by the physiologist applies to an action that is the subject of the conclusion drawn; and it is the same occurrence except that what it is that the physiologist is discussing is now understood, no longer as an item of physiological happening, but as an action. Such an understanding of the proceedings is possible only by placing that proceeding in the context appropriate to human actions; and because this is done motives, reasons, intentions and justifications now have a relevant role. But the description given in the conclusion that someone unknown killed Smith by shooting him is itself a matter of fact description with respect to which a matter of moral fact, namely murder, can be argued. For some-one killing Smith by shooting him is murder only in the appro-priate circumstances. In one such set of circumstances, it may be the act of a soldier on the battlefield who may (circumstances again being appropriate) deserve special commendation. In another context it is the action of a person who has been subjected to extreme provocation and whose action is therefore describable not as murder but in some other way that makes clear the much lesser offence involved in the action. In still another, it is the action of a person who has contempt for the life of another human being and whose action is properly describable as 'wilful and deliberate'. These are all statements of facts, they all involve descriptions of one sort or another and if the term 'matter of fact' is to be applied to any of these statements, it will be applied, not to one and only one of them, but to any one of these depending upon the particular contrast in mind and the specific matter at issue.

It is important to notice that how we shall justify or condemn an action will depend upon the character of the description given of it, i.e. upon what it is that the action is taken to be. The justification of the soldier's act of killing can be given in terms of complex matters of social and military fact, consequences and necessities, perhaps merely in terms of orders actually issued by his superior. The condemnation of the murderer's act—now described as the wilful and deliberate killing of another human being—is *not* a matter that pertains to the consequences of this sort of act; for the act that is condemned is the act described as the wilful and deliberate killing of another human being, and the character of the act as revealed in its description makes plain the extremity of the moral offence. This is not to deny that there are nice questions of moral and social consequences that may arise in the selection of criteria to be employed for the proper application of this description. Nor is it to deny that an action described in a different way may require for its moral appraisal a consideration of the consequences of that particular act or of acts so described. Here *everything* depends upon what the act is, and this can only be determined by reflecting upon what description can be given of it, as to whether or not consequences are relevant to a determination of its rightness. Here the analogy with the considerations mentioned in the case of 'the right chess-move' is of crucial importance. And just as in that case the question of the application of 'right' to a move can only be determined by reference to the object of the game (winning or avoiding defeat), so in the moral case whether or not an action is called 'right' will be determined, but in different ways depending upon what kinds of actions are under review, by the overriding consideration that the moral status of the persons concerned are preserved.

XII

We have seen that terms like 'right' and 'wrong' are rather broad terms; one would be inclined to say that they are blanket terms were it not for the fact that this suggests that there is no single overriding consideration involved in their application to the very many different sorts of actions they describe. In any case, we have seen that the question whether or not considerations of consequences are relevant to the question of the rightness of an action will depend crucially upon the description given of the action. It will not do to retort that this in effect is merely a verbal point, since whether or not a given description is applied to an action will be settled by an appeal to the consequences of the action. The counter-retort required here is 'What action?'; since what we shall take to be the action will depend upon the description we can offer of it. And instead of speaking vacuously and vaguely in the characteristic fashion of moral philosophers about consequences of action, it is imperative for clarity's sake that we recognize that what we shall take to be consequences of a given action will depend upon what we take the action to be, i.e. what description we shall apply to it. And here it is vitally important to distinguish between the action as described and the consequences of the action so described and understood.

Here it is appropriate to remark upon another related misconception. If, as I have argued, the question of the relevance of consequences to the determination of rightness will depend upon the description given, will it not follow that it is after all only a matter of arbitrary choice as to which description we shall take and hence as to whether or not consequences are to be considered? I want now to deal with this query in order to attempt to specify just what it is that is involved in the concept of the rightness of an action.

Let us return for a moment to the analogy of the chess-move. Someone who does not know the game at all and hence does not understand what is being done observes an odd-shaped physical object being pushed from one square to another on a chequered board. Someone who does know the game observes what is happening as the moving of the queen from K-4 to K-5. Someone who is more perspicuous observes what is happening as a forcing move that will render it necessary for the opponent to exchange queens. The player, however, will offer an explanation of what he is doing in terms of some complex strategy which involves but is not exhausted in the forcing move. Now each of these accounts fits what is happening on the board of play and each such account describes what is taking place—one thing is taking place that is being described in these different ways. Now, is it a matter of arbitrary choice as to which description we shall apply to the action? This, surely, is not a question about the words we shall use, for of course we can vary the locutions we employ, and which of several possible locutions to employ in offering any *given* description is a matter of choice and will be settled by preferences in matters of linguistic style. The question, rather, is which of the several possible descriptions, however it may be that one might choose to put any description in words, we shall select. But this is not a matter of verbal style or arbitrary choice, for to ask 'Which description shall we select?' is to ask, 'What did the player do?' The temptation here is to look for the 'real' doing or 'real' action as the doing or action described in one given way, and to suppose that when the doing or action is described in another way, it is this 'real' doing that is being mentioned together with some further account of it. Thus, the temptation is to suppose that when we say that the player is moving the queen from K-4 to K-5, what we are saying is that he is moving a certain kind of physical object from one square to another on a chequered board and *in addition* something else, the force of which when taken together with the statement describing the physical movement will give us the import of the statement that the player is moving the queen from K-4 to K-5. This is a familiar and very tempting sort of philosophic gambit, but it will not do at all. For nothing that follows the words 'in addition', in the preceding sentence, could possibly give us the required import except the statement that the physical object was a queen and that a chess move was being made from the squares labelled K-4 to K-5 respectively. Indeed, the account offered is manifestly false, since a player can make a move without pushing the pieces about—armless men can and do play chess, and so do persons playing blindfolded. In any case, our interest in the move described as the movement of the queen from K-4 to K-5 is not an interest in a physical happening but in a move in a game. Here, then, are once more confusions of a fundamental sort concerning the concept of an action—this time in the temptation to identify what 'really' happened with one true account of what did happen, and to look upon the other true accounts as simply introducing additional factors that need to be appended to the true and proper account of what actually occurred. To avoid such confusions, it will be useful to put the question in the following way: How shall we *understand* what has taken place when several different descriptions or accounts of what has occurred are possible? For it is the question of understanding the move that is at issue when we are asked whether or not it is a matter of choice as to which of several possible descriptions may be applied to the move.

Understanding in this case may be wholly lacking (in the case of a person who describes what has taken place as the pushing of an object from one coloured square to another, because he does not know chess), or incomplete (as in the case of a person who describes what has taken place as the move of the queen from K-4 to K-5 because he is unmindful of the strategic condition of the chess-men on the board), or as more perceptive but still inadequate (as in the case of the person who describes what has taken place as the forcing of an exchange of queens), or as complete (as in the case of a person who describes what has taken place as a forcing move that will lead, say, to a check-mate in three moves). It is the same thing that is done, that can be misunderstood and that can be understood more or less adequately as more or less of the circumstances surrounding the proceedings on the board of play are taken into account.

So it is with the alternative descriptions that can be applied to an action on the moral stage. The question whether or not the consequences of an action are relevant to its description as 'right' will depend upon the character of the description applicable to the action, but this neither implies nor asserts that we are entitled to choose whatever description we like, to assert dogmatically and on first sight, 'This is the way it strikes me—an action of such-and-such a sort' and thus to opt as we please for one rather than another procedure of moral justification. Recently there has been a good deal of misleading talk about moral commitments and of the choice of moral principles, thereby suggesting that it is all a matter of choice as to what principles if any we shall adopt. Now we may choose to do what is right and to become better men, and thus we may choose to play the moral game better or worse; and we may choose to play the moral game in the sense that we may choose to abide more frequently by moral considerations. But unlike the choice we have to play or not to play chess, and thus to play badly or well, it is not up to us to decide whether 'good' and 'bad' may be applied to our conduct any more than it is up to us whether or not we shall receive that training by which we have come to be persons endowed with some measure of moral understanding. If, then, we are persons who, in Locke's words, are 'concerned and accountable' we shall not regard the application of a description to an action as a matter of arbitrary choice; rather we shall regard alternative descriptions of an action as alternative accounts of what the action is. Here we must resist the temptation to look upon one account, as in the case of the chess-move, as the true and proper account of the action *per se*, to seek for what might be called the lowest common denominator in the series of possible descriptions of an action and to view the subsequent members of the series of descriptions as merely introducing additional factors that need to be 'tacked on' to the first and 'proper' account given. 'Giving special consideration to one's parents' is a very general description—a moral description— of an action. The action so described might also be described as 'helping them make repayment on a loan'. That same action might also be described as 'removing money from one's pocket and placing it in the hand of one of one's parents'. And this same action could also be described as 'transferring a coloured piece of paper from one's pocket to . . . etc.' And a physiologist could also describe the proceedings in his characteristic way. Not only this, but a moral agent could perhaps describe the very same action in a radically different manner as 'loaning money to one's parents', as 'giving them money one can easily spare', as 'giving them money borrowed on a false promise to repay', as 'giving them money obtained through murder' and so on indefinitely. Which shall we say is the 'real' or 'correct' account of the action? It is unnecessary to repeat what should be abundantly clear by this time, that the physiologist's account has no preferential status, indeed, that his account is not an account of a human action at all; that given our status as persons who are concerned with the moral relations in which we stand to others, relatives, friends and strangers alike, there is room for both misunderstanding and understanding of actions that can be described in such varied ways, and finally that how we shall justify an item of human action will depend upon the measure of understanding or lack of it that we have of that action.

But just how is it that we do understand an action as right? Here the morally relevant circumstances that surround and render intelligible an action are provided by the complex network of rights and obligations of the persons concerned and affected. Favouring a person, if it is done by a son towards his father, is giving one's parent special consideration. But both father and

son are described in various other ways that make clear the
variety of social roles they play in the total community, and
thereby specify the diversity of rights and obligations they have.
A person who is a father is and must also be a good many other
things as well, e.g. husband, employee, educator, automobile
driver, etc. So it is with his son. And each of these descriptive
terms indicates the social and moral role the person to whom it is
applied plays with respect to others and hence the variety of
rights, privileges and obligations which constitute his moral
position within the community. Some of these rights, privileges
and obligations may be freely assumed and freely relinquished—
a person may change his vocation, give up and obtain new
employment, take his automobile out on the public highway, and
so on—and to that extent the character of the moral roles he may
play with respect to others may be altered at will. But if it is
morally required or morally permissible that he exercise such
freedom, it is so precisely to the extent that he has obligations
and rights that are not so alterable at will: he is a responsible
moral agent, a husband or a parent or both, and these are moral
roles not so freely relinquished, if at all, which circumscribe the
area of legitimate choice which he can and does have in the matter
of his rights and obligations.

Now in the vast majority of cases very few of these rights and
obligations need to be taken into account in achieving the requisite
understanding of an action. Giving someone some special treat,
given the circumstance that the person so treated is one who has
the special right of a parent, is giving special consideration to
one's parent. The action described in the former manner *is*, in
that circumstance, the action described in the latter manner. And
in most cases in which both of these descriptions apply the
further moral description 'morally required' or 'right' will also
apply. For in most cases this sort of multiply describable action
is *not* also correctly describable as failing to meet one's obligation
to anyone else. Now given this understanding of an action, it
follows that the action is right, not because the action so described
and understood has consequences that thereby 'make' the action
right (although, that it is describable correctly in some of the ways
indicated above, is a matter with respect to which consequences
may be relevant given some relatively restricted description), but

for a quite different reason. To see this, consider the case in which a person performs some friendly act with respect to someone who is in fact his friend; and let us suppose that this friendship is desirable. Now it would be a mistake to suppose that the friendly action in this case is right because it produces friendship (something we have supposed to be worth having); although in some other case it might be correct to say that a friendly action would be right because it would promote friendship or, possibly, lead to friendship. Granted that friendship is desirable, the friendly action of A with respect to his friend B is right *because it is a friendly action—the action of one friend to another*—and as such maintains the friendly relations between the two persons. Similarly, given the moral status of a parent with respect to his son (and surely it is analytic that it is right that this moral relation be preserved) the considerate action of the latter with respect to the former, which is not a case of a failure to meet any other obligation the latter may have, is in the same way the right action—not because of any consequences it may have, but because it is the action it is, namely, the action of a son towards his father. So understood, the action is understood to be right, for it is this kind of action that maintains the moral relations of the persons concerned. It is in this sense that it serves and preserves the moral roles of the parties concerned. To put it in other words, the action is understood to be right because it is understood to be the characteristic action of one whose status with respect to that of another is that of son to father. In this given case this is all that is involved in the understanding of the action as right.

Of course where the moral relations between father and son are unsatisfactory, i.e. where the moral status of each with respect to the other can be improved, the consideration-giving action of a son may help matters, just as a friendly action may encourage and make for friendship. But here the notion of consequences is not the typical version offered by moral philosophers, which may apply to the consequences of physical events in nature but surely does not apply to this vastly different sort of case. In any case the consideration-giving action of a son, in this instance, will be understood to be right precisely to the extent to which it promotes the moral relations of the parties concerned so that, given such relations in which father and son play their characteristic moral roles with respect to each other, it will be possible for a son to act in such a way that his action can be properly described as the action of a son towards his father. Hence, in the present case, what is central is the sort of understanding of an action described in the previous paragraph.

Notoriously, there are the hard and sometimes very difficult cases in which rights and obligations compete for satisfaction, in which not every moral status of the persons concerned can be served by one's action, and in which one must of necessity exercise choice. The action described as giving special consideration to one's father is, in this enlarged context of rights and obligations, describable perhaps as the failure to keep a promise, or as the sacrifice of one's own talents, or as the failure to meet one's obligation to one's wife or to one's own children, and so on. Here disagreement sometimes but not invariably arises as to how best to deal with the practical problem posed; and even where it occurs it need not, given the moral understanding of the persons concerned (which may or may not be assisted by explanations offered by the agent), mar or destroy the moral relations of any of the affected parties. For the task of moral understanding in such cases is that of understanding the character of the action performed by viewing it in the context of the relevant rights and obligations of all of the parties concerned; and even where differences in such understanding remain unresolved, mutual respect and acknowledgment of the moral status of the other party to the disagreement can and often do remain unimpaired. What is essential to the determination of the rightness of the given course of action, no less than to the mutual respect that may defy differences about any action, is the maintenance of the moral structure of the relations between all of the parties concerned.

At this point it may be asked, what, however, is meant by the 'rightness', the 'moral requiredness' of an action, and how does this feature connect with the manner in which an action serves this moral structure? Here I shall be very brief: It is self-evident—analytic—that it is right that one maintain the moral community of which one is a member. To be right is the very same thing as to be the kind of action that does serve, however that may be, the moral community. There is no further feature over and above this one that is the rightness and that needs to be connected with it.

XIII

It will be remembered that in section II, two problems were raised. We have now dealt with the second one that has to do with the manner in which the right of a parent to special consideration can justify the relevant obligation-meeting conduct as right, morally required or obligatory. I turn now to the problem postponed in that section for later discussion, namely, how it is that this right 'derives' from a person's parental status. I shall now argue that the force of the problem rests on a misconception, that the parental status in question *is* the moral role or status of the parent, and that the special right in question just *is* this moral status of the parent with respect to his offspring.

It should come as no surprise that the difficulty expressed in the question 'How can the matter of fact parental status of a person provide a basis for his special right?' lies in a misconception, widespread in contemporary moral philosophy, of the use of the expression 'matter of fact'. This misconception is not peculiar to moral philosophy. It occurs frequently in the writings of philosophers of art. Indeed, it can arise with respect to the account that can be given of any action whether or not it is the object of moral review. One might, for example, argue that the 'matter of fact' involved in making a gift consists simply in executing some bodily movement and then go on to contrast this matter of fact with the matter of 'gift fact' (for making a gift must surely be distinguished from moving the gift object from, say, one's pocket to the palm of the recipient's hand). Or, one might just as well say that since pushing a peculiarly shaped object from one square to another on a chequered board must be distinguished from making a chess-move (infants can do the former but not the latter), one must distinguish between this matter of fact and the matter of chess fact. Moral philosophy has no monopoly on the misconception concerning the use of the term 'matter of fact', namely, the supposition that there is some absolute or intrinsic matter-of-factness about some matters and that the descriptions given of these pure matters of fact enjoy this same privileged status as proper descriptions. This piece of bad metaphysics comes down to us, ironically enough, from Hume;

and while it is a fundamental article of faith in a good deal of contemporary analytic philosophy so-called, it will not withstand inspection.

If we reflect on the matter it will be clear that there are matters of fact *and* matters of fact, descriptions *and* descriptions, of all sorts. These items cover a wide variety of very different sorts of things. What is the absolute or intrinsic matter-of-factness involved in being a parent? Let us begin by considering as a candidate for pristine purity of description the account given by a genealogist who investigates in some sort of empirical fashion the natural relations between individuals and who displays these factual matters in his elaborate charts of family trees. But now this is puzzling, for how can the simple lineal relation that holds between a father and his son provide any basis for, or render intelligible, the fact of morality, namely, that the father has a right *vis-à-vis* his son? Indeed, such a lineal relation might hold where it would be not only intelligible but correct to say that the former was never a father to the latter. Further, the matter of genealogical fact cannot be the unblemished or pure matter of fact we are looking for, since the lineal relations represent complex matters of social fact —the marriages of the persons referred to are indicated, and this alone presents a crack in a dike erected to prevent the intrusion of 'nondescriptive' matters. Would it not be safer to say that the real matter of fact consists in this fact that the individual labelled 'father' fertilized the ovum produced by the individual labelled 'mother', from which in turn the individual labelled 'son' developed? Unfortunately, all other difficulties aside, words like 'father', 'mother' and 'son' are not unmeaning labels but descriptive and indeed forensic terms, in Locke's use of this word. Should we not go one step further and speak about the matters of purely embryological fact in order to obtain the required purity of fact? But if we do this, we shall gain a matter of fact only at the expense of changing the subject, for we shall no longer be discussing fathers and their sons, nor rights and obligations, nor even actions that can be properly described as right or wrong. Although matters of sexual fact, no less than matters of social fact, are logically involved in our concept of a father, such considerations of embryology are no part of the meaning of 'father'; they are, rather, interesting and important matters that have been discovered about the mechanism of procreation. And while this embryological account applies no doubt to persons we call fathers (for we do accept as true the accounts embryologists offer of the facts with which they are concerned) this is not the matter of fact with which we, as distinct from embryologists, are concerned when we describe a person as a father.

The expression 'matter of fact' does have, of course, a legitimate use in our discourse, but only as a relative term. What will count as a matter of fact will depend wholly upon what is at issue. A relevant matter of fact with respect to the question whether or not A obtained some object as a gift from B is the fact that B placed that object in A's hand, uttering the words 'This is for you'. A relevant matter of fact with respect to the question whether or not A made his move during a game of chess is the fact that A pushed one of the pieces from one square to another. And a relevant matter of fact with respect to the question whether or not A has a right to special consideration from B is the fact that A is B's parent. But this last does not imply that with respect to the moral matter at issue, the matter of fact is itself devoid of all moral import, something that could be understood by a being wholly devoid of all moral understanding. The relevant matter of fact might have been a promise made in the past by B to A, and here the notion of a promise is a moral notion. What will count as a matter of fact will depend therefore upon the matter at issue, and what will count in a given case as a matter of fact with respect to a moral matter at issue may itself be a matter of moral fact, with respect to which in turn other matters of fact, moral or not, may be cited.

Consider the relations holding between the following matters of fact. Let A be the immediate forebear of B. Then a matter of embryological fact applies. The latter matter of fact has to do with the causal mechanism involved in the birth of B, and because we accept the findings of embryologists, we say that these matters are always present whenever there are the matters of fact with which genealogists are concerned, namely, the facts of sex, marriage (if absent, the offspring will be labelled 'illegitimate') and birth. This, indeed, apart from matters having to do with the identities of the individuals concerned (A is identified as William Warren, baker; B as John Warren, legislator), is all that is involved in a typical account offered by a genealogist; and hence the concept of A as a person who has a right with respect to B simply has no place in this account. This does not mean that genealogists are unconcerned in their capacity as genealogists with moral matters. This much of course is true. It means, rather, that in circumstances confined wholly to these matters of genealogical fact questions of rights and obligation are as much out of place as questions of gifts and bequests would be in circumstances in which there was no private property at all, and just as much so as questions of whether or not chess moves had been made in the case in which an infant had pushed chessmen about on a chequered board. Hence the genealogist's use of terms like 'parent', 'father', 'mother' and 'son' are logically impoverished or anaemic, since these terms are now stripped of their logical connection with such moral terms as 'rights', 'obligation', etc. It is true that the conception of marriage figures in the genealogical table, in order that the distinction between legitimate and illegitimate offspring might be made, but marriage is considered in this context only as legal or contractual relation. The conception of family life in which there is cooperation and the mutual acknowledgment of interests, in which concerns, needs, hopes, desires, aspirations and so on operate in the community of the family, and in the context of which it does make sense to speak of privileges and responsibilities, rights and obligations—all of these matters have been stripped away from the matters of fact represented on the genealogical chart. But let these matters of family fact be introduced as circumstances surrounding the individuals designated on this chart, and the individuals become parents and offspring who are a good deal more than biological entities or legal persons. In these circumstances, they are social and moral agents with their distinctive social and moral roles which words like 'father' and 'son' ordinarily convey. In this full-fledged sense to speak of A as the father of B is not to remark on a matter of genealogical fact, but rather on a matter of social and moral fact, the status of A with respect to B in the complex circumstances of family life.

In any account of the affairs within the family circle, it is altogether necessary that we distinguish between matters of morality and matters that pertain to manners, habits, personal

F

idiosyncrasies, love and affection. To think of the relations of persons within the family as dictated wholly or primarily by considerations of moral matters, is to think of the family as excessively harsh and constricted. Where there is the tendency to make a moral issue of the relations between members of a family, there the point of the family life—the happiness of its members— is missed as love and affection are supplanted by an excessive moralism. This indeed is the objection to Puritanism in family life—it blights the happiness of the persons concerned which after all does give the family its point as a social institution. Further there are matters of local custom, habits and personal idiosyncrasy in the affairs of any family, which are recognized and acknowledged as such and to which, within limits, due recognition and assent are and should be given by the members of the family. But here again there can be excess and tyranny which sometimes blight the relations and the lives of persons in the family or which, even if they give rise to no discord, crystallize matters of purely local custom or habit into articles of moral dogma. Mistaken notions no less than aberrant practices can and sometimes do blight the thoughts and the lives of members of a family.

How then shall we distinguish in these affairs between moral and non-moral matters? Here it is altogether unhelpful to resort to what appears to me to be the essential obscurantism of the intuitionist's move: the talk about the 'moral' and the 'non-moral' meanings of terms, as if one could tell from a kind of direct inspection of objects on just what matters these labels should be pasted. Further, this line suggests that the distinction between moral and non-moral matters is hard and fast; but there is no sharp boundary between matters of moral import and *mere* matters of local manners and customs. Whether or not a given practice is a matter in which moral concern may be taken will depend upon the view taken of the central importance of the practice to the preservation of the life of the family. It is for this reason that rights and obligations, privileges and responsibilities are distributed in familiar ways to the members of a family in accordance with their several roles. Specifically, it is for this reason that the status of a parent, a father, is invested with moral significance. For that status whether explicitly recognized as moral or not, is a moral status precisely because it is essential to the continued existence of the family community. It is true that the loss of a father may not be altogether destructive of family life, but at best only an unsatisfactory makeshift can be contrived. For without the status within the family of the father, there cannot be the effective distribution of love and affection that provides for the happiness of all concerned, nor the matter of local customs and habits that regulate the conduct of the members of the family with respect to one another. A family bound together very largely and consciously so by moral ties may be inferior to one in which common affairs are softened and enhanced by affection and love, but so far at least it can endure and render possible the minimal amenities and advantages afforded to individuals through their participation in the life of the family. Hence it is that no clear-cut distinction can be drawn between matters of morality and matters of manners and local custom: what may appear to be local custom may in the specific circumstances of family life be of vital importance to its preservation. In these matters there are, of course, degrees; and inevitably there will be border-line cases that cannot be described decisively and clearly either as matters of mere custom or as matters of morality.

'Father' (and so too with 'mother', 'parent', etc.) marks the social role of a person within a complex institutional arrangement, in which he and others participate, and to which in their distinctive ways they contribute. The moral character of that role has to do with its central importance to the continuing existence of a family in which all participate and flourish. That social role, however, is not exclusively moral in character; and for this reason I referred to the social *and* moral import of words like 'parent' and 'father'. If we are to say, then, that it is in virtue of A's parental status that A has the right he has, we must not suppose that we are thereby calling attention to something other than the right he has from which in turn the right is derived. On the contrary, to say this is to *identify* the right as the moral role that A plays with respect to B. This does not imply that A and B must be continuing participants in a family life. Families do dissolve and children do grow up and leave the circle of the family. But as long as something of the character of the relation that does exist within the family remains in the relation between A and B, then A will have a right and B the correlative obligation, not because of past benefits received by B from A, but because A remains in important respects B's parent. To say, then, that it is by virtue of A's parental status with respect to B that he has the right to special consideration from B is to explain the right by identifying it; it is not to derive the right from anything alien to it—it is to provide a place for that right on the complex map of rights and obligations, duties and responsibilities by reference to which the persons concerned may be guided in their thought and action, their expectations, hopes and desires.

Were we to see one person, B, give special consideration in his action to another, A, we might then ask, 'By what right does A enjoy such special favour from B?' To be told that 'A is B's parent' is to be given a good and sufficient reason for the claim that A has that right; for this reply makes clear the character of the moral relation between A and B. It would be superfluous to add that parents have a right to special consideration from their sons and daughters. For the answer given explains the moral status of parents and as such explains the right in question; the additional remark would be employed in teaching someone the moral use of the term 'parent', but where this use is understood it is otiose. Here my comments parallel those made in connection with the so-called rule 'One ought to give special consideration to one's parents'. For the word 'parent' in itself when employed in the context of a discussion of a right makes clear the moral role of the person to whom it is applied. To say then that it is the parental status of a given person that guarantees the right he enjoys is to make clear that it is in the capacity of his parental role rather than that of any other moral role (e.g. as the recipient of a promise) that he is entitled to the treatment he receives. If this account is correct, justifying the claim that A has a right to special consideration from B, and thereby meeting the challenge 'By what right . . .?' in no way involves consideration of the consequences of the special consideration given. For whether or not the *action* by which A is favoured is right (and to this question consequences may or may not be relevant depending, as we have seen, upon the correct account or description given of the action), the right that A has is the right that *is* his moral status or role with respect to B. For it is only when A, the immediate forebear of B, stands in the appropriate moral relation to B, that A has the requisite moral status, i.e. that A has the parental right in question and B the filial obligation to A which he can meet only by giving A special consideration. Justifying the claim that A has a special right to the treatment B has accorded him consists in explaining the person A by specifying his moral status with respect to B.

At this point, perhaps, it may be objected that no elucidation has yet been given of the right as such, that all that has been done so far is somehow to relate this right to the status or role of the person who *has* the right, that the account of this status is as yet obscure, and that an adequate characterization of this moral role must make specific mention of certain peculiarly moral or normative properties. It is this last sort of consideration that has led many writers to say that the conception of a person having a right either entails (or is logically equivalent to) the conception of the person's 'absolute', 'intrinsic', 'infinite value'—the thought that he is 'priceless but without price'.

As moral rhetoric these familiar locutions can be highly effective, but in philosophy edification has no place at all and too often conceals our intellectual shortcomings from ourselves. For, like the familiar talk about *prima facie* rights, these older ways of speaking substitute verbal slogans for the clear and difficult thinking required in philosophy.

Yet there *is* something important in this talk about the intrinsic value of the human person, vague and frightfully muddled as this sort of talk is. Our whole attitude to, our whole way of talking about and dealing with, a human being is radically different from that involved in our relations with material objects, different even from that involved in our dealings with animals. Indeed, there is something horrible in the accounts that have come down to us of the attempts of some of the Cartesians to demonstrate how remarkably complex are those mechanisms called 'cats' and 'dogs' by the vulgar—how incredibly amazing that such mechanisms should make such noises when sharp instruments are stuck into them! There is something horrible in these 'experiments' for here our descriptions of such beings are not that they are mechanisms that make noises but animals that suffer, are frightened, squirm in agony, and so on; and these descriptions reveal something about our attitudes towards them. Try for a moment to regard one's cat or dog as a mere biological specimen, perhaps as an exasperating mechanism in the way in which one regards one's automobile when it 'misbehaves' and prevents one from keeping an appointment! This can be done, but it is shocking, and when it does it is as if the animal had ceased to be a cat or dog describable in the familiar ways. How much more true is this of human beings! Here it is scarcely possible to make this sort of brutalizing 'experiment'. The very language we employ to describe human beings and their experiences—the complex and intricate array of psychological terms[1] we employ in describing their thoughts, feelings, emotions, moods and actions —reveals something about our attitudes to other human beings; our attitudes towards them are attitudes to personalities, if one wishes, to souls. And of course, our attitude to a personality, to another soul, is radically different from our attitude to a physical object, which we can use as a tool. But to set forth the character of this difference between human beings and physical objects in terms of an 'infinite intrinsic value' ascribable to the former but never to the latter is not only to engage in edification but also to play fast and loose with words. Indeed this way of talking rests upon a serious misconception of the difference it is designed to explain. It involves the radical muddle, that if one could somehow see through the veil of external bodily phenomena (the spoken words, the facial and bodily movements) into the very depths of a person's being, one would somehow find a quality of sheer preciousness in itself that endows a human being with his status as the possessor of a right.

Here, once again, the misconceptions that obscure the use of psychological terms, a use with which all of us are familiar in the recognition and in the descriptions we offer of the character of human experiences—feelings, emotions, moods, desires, hopes and so on, create havoc in moral philosophy. Of course we can describe the moral status of a person as the possessor of the right to special consideration from his son! Our vocabulary is quite adequate for this purpose. To do so we need only describe the character of the lives typical of those who are related, as fathers and sons are within the life of a family that succeeds in achieving the point of the institution. Here we need to attend to the manner

---

[1] By 'psychological terms' I do not mean, of course, certain words as these are used by psychologists, but the familiar uses of words to describe mental phenomena.

in which concerns and cares, hopes and aspirations, needs, desires and interests—the list could easily be expanded—operate within the flourishing life of the family community and mark the complex character of the relations of father to son without which that common enterprise cannot be served and preserved. And this, in part, is precisely what an effective novelist does when he takes the paternal relation as the subject of his literary portrayal. To describe this matter of moral fact is to describe the moral character of the relation of father to son, to show how a responsible and solicitous father regards his son and to reveal something of the attitude of a person to his father. Here we do have an account of moral attitudes, of the moral status of a father, and of his son, without invoking some inner normative and mysterious property of the person the possession of which by the person is then thought to be his moral status as the possessor of a right. The search for such a property rests upon the failure to understand the character of the psychological concepts employed in the description of persons, their thoughts, feelings, emotions, desires, interests, etc.

This is scarcely the place for the large scale and detailed inquiry into the character of the psychological concepts which must be employed in any detailed description of the moral status of a father in relation to his son, but a number of rather general observations may be in order at this point.

Mention was made above of the cares and concerns, the needs and interests that give substance to the moral relation of father and son, and one could go on to speak about the essential role of the father in the growth and development of his son, the manner in which the former cares for, sustains and contributes in diverse indispensable ways to the development of the latter. In such an account, a number of psychological terms are employed. Now there is nothing intrinsically *moral* about these terms, neither is there anything intrinsically non-moral about them. Their import, whether moral or not, will depend upon the particular circumstances or context in which they are employed. The word 'need' can be employed by an artist concerned to obtain needed materials for his work, e.g. canvas or oil-paint; by an art critic in judging the merits of a work in progress ('The painting needs more contrast at this point'); by a child who needs a shovel with which to

build its sand castle; by a parent who needs a job in order to provide for his family; by a mother who tells her son that he needs to
be more considerate of the wishes of his father; and so on indefinitely. The psychological terms employed in describing the
moral status of a parent, a father, can be used in moral as well as
in non-moral matters, and when they are used in moral contexts
their use is then moral in character. To suppose that there is
some sort of intrinsic moral neutrality about psychological terms
is to relapse into the kind of mistake so frequently made about the
term 'matter of fact', which I have been at considerable pains to
expose.

Most importantly, psychological terms that are employed in the
description of the moral status of a parent are not theoretical
terms designed to describe or refer to the inaccessible interior
mental happenings of other people, a private glimpse of which
we are privileged to have in the case of ourselves; they are, rather,
practical terms whose use we come to grasp by learning how to
employ them in our practical affairs, whether this be in splashing
paint on a canvas, building sand castles on the beach, or in dealing
with other human beings in various sorts of ways. Hence it is
that the criteria for their proper application to other persons are
quite often many and complex, and hence too the possibility in
some cases of the honest mistakes we make when we apply them
to ourselves. Again, this is the explanation of the fact that our
attitudes to other human beings as human beings, not as sticks
and stones, machines, or tools, is so intimately connected with the
employment of these terms in our discourse about other human
beings; for the use of these terms is learned when, as children, we
learn to deal practically with other human beings. It is this background of practical relations with other human beings that provides the logical support upon which our understanding of
psychological and social terms rests. It is for this reason, finally,
that moral uses of psychological terms are possible; for when
these terms are employed in our discourse about matters which
are of basic importance to the maintenance and security of the
communities in which we live, that discourse can and does
function morally no less than factually. Moral philosophers, in
the accounts they have given of the moral uses of terms, have
been too much preoccupied with moral verdicts, with their

employment in passing judgement upon the decencies and indecencies in the character and conduct of individuals. Hence it is that certain words like 'right', 'wrong', 'duty', 'good', 'bad', etc., have been thought to be peculiarly adapted to moral discourse. But when an account of the moral status of a person is given by means of such words as 'needs', 'interests', 'concern', etc., which are not included in the limited moral vocabulary of moral philosophers, the matter at issue is no less moral than matters of the decencies and indecencies that can be ascribed to persons and their conduct. Here, no less than in the case of the concept of an action, misunderstandings of the ways in which psychological terms are used plays havoc with discussions in moral philosophy.

All of this, however, may not settle the mind of one who wants to know just what the right as such is. A right is something a person *has*, whatever his status may *be*. What then is this right as such? The query rests on a misconception. The right of a parent is no proprietary article—a kind of mystic moral badge worn by the parents. Neither is the right of a chess player some magical possession he can trot out for inspection that has as its remarkable issue the move which, as we would say, he has a right to make. If we think of a parent's right as something of the order of an object in his or her possession, then we shall be led to think of it as something mental. Indeed, failing to find this mental object, we shall be led to follow those who regard a right as a fictitious entity eminently suitable as a fiction for social purposes; or, borrowing Hume's language from his discussion of the analogous case of promises, we shall speak of a right as '*naturally* something altogether unintelligible'.[1] But it is surely unnecessary to introduce such remarkable bits of self-deception in order to explain our moral beliefs. I mentioned the case of the chess player who has a right to make the move he makes, in order to focus attention upon the character of the misconception—for here, and precisely because of the artificiality of the game situation, everything is in view. Hence we are not tempted, as one might be in the case of the moral right, to look for a mysterious interior object identifiable as the right. To say that the chess player has the right is to say that he is entitled to move, and this is understandable in

[1] *A Treatise of Human Nature*, Bk. III, Pt. II, Sec. V.

terms of his status within the context of the game—he is a player
and performs his role as a player during the course of play.
Similarly to say that a parent has a right to special consideration
from his son or daughter is to describe one facet of the complex
role that a parent has within the life of a family. Specifically, it is
to describe in a very general way, as we have seen, the kind of
conduct of the offspring necessary to the maintenance of an aspect
of the moral role a parent plays in the life of the family, a role that
is essential to the moral community of the family, which in turn
is essential to the total moral community of which the family is a
part. To set forth this role of the parent with respect to his or her
offspring, we need have no recourse to mysterious properties or
possessions of the parents—the right *is* that role.

XIV

In this brief concluding section I want to offer a number of
cautions and comments about the character of the argument just
concluded.

First, there is an objection that needs to be considered. Is
not all of this a blow for conservatism, the *status quo*, the per-
petuation of our common social institutions and ordinary moral
prejudices? This is an absurd objection, although it is properly
directed perhaps against some view not here adumbrated. Nevertheless it does touch upon matters of considerable importance of
which we need to be reminded.

In section VII I remarked that morality is self-correcting.
The common social life which gives meaning to our moral discourse is itself subject to change and transformation. There is
no doubt that even within the moral life of the family, important
changes have been wrought in the specific moral relations between
parents and offspring by industrial growth and development of
knowledge and technology. The specific ways in which a son
may meet his obligation to his parents are subject to change, and

the specific occasions on which parents may be justified in the exercise of their parental rights are subject to variation. When for example, education becomes an extremely complex matter that may no longer be left to the jurisdiction and judgement of parents, the right of a parent may be limited by matters of the social necessities of a complex society, as indeed it is in the matter of the minimum permissible schooling of children. This indeed is wise and proper, for the moral relations in which persons within the family stand to one another are circumscribed by the moral features of a common moral life served by the family. But, in addition, the morality, whether of the family or of the community as a whole, does have a point. Let me return briefly to an already overworked analogy. The justification that may be given of particular moves made during a chess game are one thing, the point of playing, namely, the enjoyable exercise of a sophisticated intellectual skill is another; but there is nothing to prevent changes being introduced into the character of the game and hence into the character of justifications that may be given of moves that are made, in order better to serve the point of the game. So it is in the case of morality. The character of the moral relations in which persons stand to one another and hence of the justifications that can be offered of conduct must be understood by reference to the actual moral relations in which agents stand to one another within such institutions as the family, and if the word will please a hostile critic of the argument presented in this essay, I shall admit to some prejudice in favour of the institution of the family. But morality has a point as well as a content—the achievement, for those who participate in the moral life, of the diverse forms of happiness possible for moral agents. Given this point of our morality, critical scrutiny and reappraisals of moral institutions and relations are not only possible, but during times of social change consequent upon increased knowledge and technological development, they are altogether necessary.

It would carry us beyond the scope of this discussion to elaborate further upon the point of morality as expressed above. Our interest here is the character of the moral relations of parents to their offspring, and nothing so far said may be construed as an endorsement of the traditional muddles of utilitarianism either on the psychology of pleasure or on the confusion of the meaning of a moral utterance with the point of moral utterances in general. But these are large questions and both call for extended and difficult examination not possible within the limits of this inquiry.

Another comment. For those whose morality has been conceived of as a matter having to do with the commands of God, the remarks made in this section do present an altered moral picture; and, no doubt, they do present altered conceptions of *duty*, *right*, *obligation*, etc. This, however, is neither surprising nor objectionable; for it is an old story, however difficult it may be to tell it in all its detail, that concepts are sometimes modified by altered opinions or acquired knowledge. Here it is fruitless to argue that, since old terms like 'morality', 'duty', 'right', 'obligation' and so on, no longer have the special overtones which they had in another day, or even to-day for others for whom an older cultural climate still lingers on, they must or should be abandoned and new ones introduced. This is a profound mistake that ignores the continuity (the growth, if one prefers) of our social and moral life. Where in the past 'right' served as a simple term to mark conduct commanded by God, it now serves as a general term applied to conduct justified sometimes in terms of consequences (in the sense appropriate to human action), sometimes not. In any case it is a term that is given unity in the diverse ways in which it is applied by reference to an overriding concern of moral agents with conduct in so far as it serves and preserves a moral life in which all of us participate in ways that are both common and diverse and in which in varied ways human beings can achieve some measure of their appropriate forms of happiness.

One final comment. I have, during the course of the argument in this and in previous sections, offered analogies which have drawn attention to problems, obscurities and confusions that are by no means peculiar to morality. I have done so deliberately in order to call attention to mistakes of a fundamental kind about the concept of an action and about other concepts, psychological and non-psychological, with which this concept is logically connected. These matters of crucial importance for moral philosophy have been ignored and brushed aside, all too frequently, in the excessively edifying but obscuring talk about the 'moral' use of this or that term. It is no wonder that moral philosophers have engaged in so much loose talk in their writings and in their discussions about actions, consequences, motives, justification, causes, etc. Until recognition of the confusion surrounding these concepts is achieved, no clarity in moral philosophy is even remotely possible. One of my objects has been to focus attention upon these fundamental but neglected problems.